The Unitarian Universalist
Pocket Guide

The Unitarian Universalist Pocket Guide

Edited by
William G. Sinkford

Fourth Edition
Skinner House Books
Boston

Published by Skinner House Books, an imprint of the Unitarian Universalist Association.

Cover design by Kimberly Glyder.

Printed in Canada.

07 06 05 04
10 9 8 7 6 5 4 3 2 1

ISBN 1-55896-478-9

Library of Congress Cataloging-in-Publication Data

Unitarian Universalist pocket guide / edited by William G. Sinkford.— 4th ed.
        p. cm.
    Includes bibliographical references.
    ISBN 1-55896-478-9 (alk. paper)
 1. Unitarian Universalist Association. I. Sinkford, William. II. Unitarian
Universalist Association.
BX9841.3.U55 2004
289.1'32—dc22

                                                                        2004008926

Contents

Preface   ix
William G. Sinkford

Our Faith   1
William F. Schulz

Our Ministry   7
Jane Ranney Rzepka

Our Worship   15
Mark Belletini

Our Religious Education   27
Makanah Elizabeth Morriss

Our Work for Social Justice and Diversity   39
Jacqui James and Meg Riley

Sharing Our Faith: Two Perspectives   49
    William Sinkford and Kay Montgomery

Our Roots   57
    Harry Scholefield and Paul Sawyer

Important Dates in Unitarian Universalist History   73

About the Unitarian Universalist Association   89

About the Church of the Larger Fellowship   93

Resources   97

Unitarian Universalist Principles

We, the member congregations of the Unitarian Universalist Association, covenant to affirm and promote:

> The inherent worth and dignity of every person;
> Justice, equity, and compassion in human relations;
> Acceptance of one another and encouragement to spiritual growth in our congregations;
> A free and responsible search for truth and meaning;
> The right of conscience and the use of the democratic process within our congregations and in society at large;
> The goal of world community with peace, liberty, and justice for all;
> Respect for the interdependent web of all existence of which we are a part.
>
> *—from the Bylaws of the Unitarian Universalist Association*

Preface

If you are reading this, perhaps you've just discovered Unitarian Universalism and want to learn a bit about this liberal faith to see if it might be right for you. Or perhaps you've been attending a Unitarian Universalist congregation and are considering becoming a member. It could be that this *Pocket Guide* is being used in an adult education class or leadership training experience in which you have enrolled. Or perhaps you've been a member of a Unitarian Universalist congregation for years and are looking for help in describing our faith because, more and more often, you are being asked to describe our "uncommon denomination."

Whatever the reason, and wherever you are on your personal religious journey, this small volume can be a valuable resource. In it, you will find no creed of belief to which you must subscribe to be a Unitarian Universalist, no statement of doctrine. Unitarian Universalists value the individual spiritual journey and believe that there is no one right way to lead a religious life. For us, religion is ultimately not about what you think. Religion is about how you live. Ours is a faith of deeds, not creeds.

Our focus on action does not mean that we do not value thought. There is perhaps no faith community that affirms more completely the power and potential of women and men to find and/or create meaning. Nor is there a religious community whose religious thought and practice are more diverse. It is typical in our congregations for liberal Christians, humanists, Buddhists, pagans, and persons whose religious beliefs are less clearly defined to sit side by side in the same pew. Many religious streams water our souls. Many spiritual practices nurture our spirits.

What we share is our commitment to the religious journey. We know that "revelation is not sealed." The wisdom and teachings of all the world's great faith traditions are resources for us. But our relationship with the holy rests in the human heart, however we may name the sacred in our lives.

What brings us together is our commitment to community, to the church. We call ours a "covenantal tradition." When we covenant with one another, we promise to walk together on our journey. A covenant is a promise to be faithful.

The very pluralism of belief that may seem a weakness is actually our great strength. In a world where racial, cultural, and religious diversity is a reality, Unitarian Universalists know, because we live it every week, that our differences need not divide us, that they are blessings rather than curses.

Because each Unitarian Universalist congregation is independent, each has its own covenant. But many congregations use some variation of the following covenant:

Love is the doctrine of this church,
The quest for truth is its sacrament,
And service is its prayer.

To dwell together in peace,
To seek knowledge in freedom,
To serve human need,

To the end that all souls shall
Grow into harmony with the divine—

Thus do we covenant with each other.

Many people who first enter a Unitarian Universalist
congregation respond by saying, "I never thought I'd find a
church where I could bring all of myself, my strengths and
my weaknesses, my answers and my questions, through the
doors." If you are one of these people, let me extend a sincere
welcome. Welcome to the religious home you may have
thought you'd never find.

The word *religion* comes from *religare,* which means to bind
together that which has been sundered. It is about the making
and re-making of connections. It is about naming the holy in our
lives and answering the call to work for healing and wholeness.

Unitarian Universalists have a proud history of working
for justice. From the abolition movement to the women's
movement, from the Civil Rights movement for persons of
color to the current civil rights movement for bisexual, gay,
lesbian, and transgender persons, Unitarian Universalists have
been in the forefront.

But the making of justice does not define our faith. Rather,
our faith calls us to work for justice. That faith is grounded in
the two great liberal traditions that came together in 1961 to
form the Unitarian Universalist Association. From the Unitarian side of the family tree, we hold that there is one spirit
of life, one promise of love, one power of human possibility,
one God. And from the Universalist tradition of salvation for
everyone, we know we must work to leave no one behind.
Unitarian Universalism stands on the side of love.

Treat this *Pocket Guide* as an introduction to some compan-
ions on your religious journey. Here you will learn something of
the story of Unitarian Universalism, something of our values,
our worship life, and our practices as a covenantal community.

You will meet Rev. William F. Schulz, former president of the Unitarian Universalist Association, who writes of our beliefs, commitments, and traditions.

Rev. Jane Ranney Rzepka is minister of the Church of the Larger Fellowship, which serves individuals who live out our faith in places where there is no established congregation.

Rev. Mark Belletini writes about worship. Mark chaired the commission that developed our current hymnbook, *Singing the Living Tradition*.

Rev. Makannah Morriss writes about our approach to religious education, which focuses on values and honors asking questions rather than learning answers.

Jacqui James and Rev. Meg Riley write about our calling to work against the oppressions that punish people for who they are.

I offer a short piece on sharing our faith. And Kay Montgomery, executive vice president of the Unitarian Universalist Association, explains that people who convert to Unitarian Universalism don't have to give up who they are.

Rev. Harry Scholefield and Rev. Paul Sawyer write as historians of our movement and its spirit.

Thank you for picking up this fourth edition of the *UU Pocket Guide*. If you want to find a UU congregation in your area or other information, please visit our website at www.uua.org, or call our Office of Information and Public Witness at (617) 742-2100, extension 131.

May this short volume be of help to you on your religious journey.

Rev. William G. Sinkford
President (2001-2005)
Unitarian Universalist Association
Of Congregations

Our Faith

Andrei Sakharov, the renowned Russian physicist, once asked his wife, Elena Bonner, "Do you know what I love most of all in life?" "I expected," Bonner confided some years later to a friend, "that he would say something about a poem or a sonata or even about me. But no. Instead, he said, 'The thing I love most in life is radio background emanation'"—the barely discernible radio waves which reach us here on earth from outer space and reflect unknown cosmic processes that ended billions of years ago.

What Sakharov meant of course was that he loved the mysteries that the cosmos hands us, the grandeur and immensity of this thing we call Creation. And he loved the fact that we human beings can occasionally get a glimpse of those mysteries and that grandeur, even the parts whose work was done billions of years ago.

Very few of us can ask the kind of sophisticated questions of the universe that an Andrei Sakharov did. Even fewer have the opportunity to receive a hint of a reply. But most of us at one time or another wonder about the ultimate questions of life: How did Time begin? Is there a God? Has life meaning? What is good? Why must we die?

These are fundamental religious questions. And most religions—at least in their orthodox varieties—believe they have the answers. Those orthodox answers may be framed in terms of Jesus Christ (Christianity), the law of the Covenant (Judaism), or the eight-fold path to Enlightenment (Buddhism), to name but three.

Unitarian Universalism is different. We respect the answers offered by Christianity, Judaism, Buddhism, and the world's other great faith traditions—we even draw our inspiration and some of our forms of worship from those traditions—but *we respect the mystery more*. We believe, in other words, that no single religion (or academic discipline, for that matter) has a monopoly on wisdom; that the answers to the great religious questions change from generation to generation; and that the ultimate truth about God and Creation, death, meaning, and the human spirit cannot be captured in a narrow statement of faith. The mystery itself is always greater than its name.

This, then, is why ours is a *creedless* faith and respect for others' beliefs is a high value. We do not require our members to subscribe to a particular theology or set of affirmations in order to join our congregations. Instead, we encourage individuals to garner insights from all the world's great faiths, as well as from Shakespeare and from science, from feminism and from feelings. We invite people to explore their spirituality in a responsible way. We ask Unitarian Universalists to cherish the earth, to free the oppressed, and to be grateful for life's blessings. Out of this combination of reflection and experience, each one of us shapes a personal faith. For Unitarian Universalists the individual is the ultimate source of religious authority.

Tradition and Community

While the individual is the ultimate source of religious authority, the individual is not the *only* source. If that were the case, Unitarian Universalists could easily fall prey to the condition that afflicted Otto von Bismarck, of whom it has been said that "he believed firmly and deeply in a God who had the remarkable faculty of always agreeing with him." No, our individual predilections need to be tempered by conversation with our tradition and tested within the crucible of our community.

Our history is important to us. Both our Unitarian and our Universalist traditions rejected the notion that "higher" authorities—be they theologians or bishops, rabbis or preachers—could impose their views upon the laity. This is the historical source of our commitment to freedom of belief, congregational polity, and lay empowerment. But our traditions also supply us with a rich legacy of positive affirmations, from Universalism's faith in the benevolence of God to Unitarianism's assurance that human beings have within them the capacity to shape the future.

The result is that today our tradition provides us with a lodestar and a sort of "early warning system" for the recognition of tenets at odds with the norms of our faith. The tradition is not definitive—it will inevitably be modified and even superseded by new "revelation"—but if you hear someone preaching hellfire and damnation or that the future is solely in the hands of God, chances are it's not a Unitarian Universalist!

And the other resource which helps shape our faith is the religious community. When I was in Hong Kong not long ago, I saw a sign in the window of a dentist's office which read, "Teeth extracted by the latest Methodists." To my knowledge, teeth extraction is not (yet) one of the things our congregations provide their members, but a supportive context within which to pursue one's religious pilgrimage certainly is. If what we discover on that pilgrimage is ever to realize its full potential, it must be shared, pondered, and tested with others.

Individual freedom of belief exists, then, in dynamic tension with the insights of our history and the wisdom of our communities. It is this tension which puts the lie to the oft-heard shibboleth that Unitarian Universalists can believe anything they like. It is true that we set up no formal religious test for legal membership, that we welcome the devout atheist as readily as the ardent Christian, but it is *not* true that one can subscribe to views at variance with our most basic values. Clearly, one could never advocate racism or genocide, for example, and still in any meaningful sense call oneself a Unitarian Universalist.

Commitments and Covenants

Though we have no creed, we surely have made covenants—with each other, with previous generations, and some would even say with God—to live as a community united around certain precepts. The most recent form of those commitments we hold in common is to be found in our Principles and Purposes. But what of those most fundamental religious questions to which I referred earlier? What does Unitarian Universalism have to teach us about God and meaning, the Good and suffering?

Obviously our answers may differ in detail depending upon our theological perspectives. Some of us would understand God in very personal ways, as the source of love or hopefulness; some would see God in nature or as Ultimate Reality; others would take the Goddess as a model; and still others would have no truck with the whole notion at all. Similarly, some of us would find life's greatest meaning through Christian prayer or Buddhist meditation; others through communion with the natural world or the pursuit of scientific understanding; and still others through the companionship of their loved ones. It is this very diversity which makes Unitarian Universalism a congenial home for those who come from different religious backgrounds.

Regardless of the details or differences, however, there are a whole host of faith affirmations with which the vast majority of us would be comfortable. Let me offer a selection. This is of course my own way of putting it, but it would, I think, be recognizable to most of my co-religionists:

- *Whatever we think the holy be, Creation itself is holy.* We make no distinctions between the natural and supernatural, the secular and sacred. We simply cherish the earth and all its creatures, the stars in all their glory.

- *Life's gifts are available to everyone, not just the Chosen or the Saved.* Only human artifice or blind ill fortune can separate us from the source of blessings. Whatever that source be, it makes no artificial distinctions among its supplicants.

- *That which is Divine (or, if you prefer, most precious and profound) is made evident, not in the miraculous or otherworldly, but in the simple and the everyday.* We look not to the heavens or an afterlife for our meaning, but to the exuberance of life's unfolding. Whatever abundance there may be is lodged right here on earth.

- *Human beings themselves are responsible for the planet and its future.* Social justice is a religious obligation. The future is never fated.

- *Every one of us is held in Creation's hand—we share its burdens and its radiance—and hence strangers need not be enemies.* The "interdependent web of all existence" offers an embrace to everything and everyone. Our only inherent enemies are violence, poverty, injustice, and oppression. The earth is our cherished home.

- *Though death confronts us all, we love life all the more even though we lose it.* An honorable and impassioned life may not deny death its due, but it can surely rob it of victory.

A Wide and Generous Faith

I am a third-generation Unitarian Universalist. This religion runs in my blood. It has spurred me and soothed me. But most Unitarian Universalists are at one time or another new-comers to our faith. Ninety percent of us come out of other religious traditions; some come from none at all. This makes for both richness and confusion.

Nonetheless, regardless of background, we each share a few fundamental convictions. Finally, let me put it this way. Too often in this world, religion has been the agent of division and fear. Unitarian Universalism seeks to heal a fractured world and the broken lives within it by calling every one of us to the best that is in us. Beyond nationalism and ethnic preju-dice, beyond materialism and greed, beyond the petty and the shallow—we invoke a global loyalty, an ecological ethic, and a deeper mercy.

In the last analysis our Unitarian Universalist mission and the faith that sustains it are clear and straightforward: *We would treat the wounds of a narrow spirit with the salve of a generous heart.* How better than that to eradicate fear? How better than that to honor life's mysteries?

William F. Schulz

Our Ministry

It is 1957. The congregation has gathered for the first annual blueberry pancake breakfast in my parents' back yard. People are talking about buying a building, looking for a minister, and mortgaging their houses to do it. Others are recalling the service they put together on Sunday about Hinduism, and how moving it was (or wasn't). One man, in tears, pours out his heart to a couple of close church friends, three old-timers pass around petitions, another small group practices a song they'll be singing together a week from Sunday—they have a ways to go. Two others are actively debating the fine points of evolution. Worker-types pour orange juice, find more plastic forks, and teach kids to flip the pancakes on the precarious homemade grills. Children tear around the yard, the teens are huddled near the pond, feeling obstinate about something, and blueberry bits are smushed all over the place. When it begins to rain, the more muscular among us try to push the first car (of a very long line) out of the mud.

Over forty years later, I read in that congregation's newsletter that the annual pancake breakfast is coming around again. Many would say that today's professional ministry is about promoting long-term community, encouraging honest and intelligent discussion, raising "good" children, developing deep friendships, working for social action, creating music, engaging in group effort, and worshipping together. But I grew up in a small congregation that did not have an ordained minister, and I know that the members of a congregation can do all of this important ministry without a professional minister.

For Unitarian Universalists, the ministry we each practice with one another results in comfort, stimulation, fun, growth, commitment to the larger good, genuine help, and religious community. Each of us ministers to the others.

Yet we credential and ordain professional ministers, too.

Beyond the Pancake Breakfast: What's a Professional Unitarian Universalist Minister For?

You may wonder just what Unitarian Universalist ministers have to offer. Imagine that you are in one of the following situations:

I no longer believe in the God of my childhood. I want to know what the great thinkers say, I want to know what my options are, and I want somebody to reassure me that it is okay to follow my theological heart's desire!

Chances are, your minister would enjoy this conversation! Credentialed Unitarian Universalist ministers have academic training and experience in a wide variety of areas, including, of course, theology. He or she may offer adult education classes, sermons, ongoing private discussion, and/or a reading list, if you are so inclined. Your minister will understand the spectrum of belief and unbelief and encourage you to find your own place.

Because Unitarian Universalists vary considerably in our individual views of spirituality, ministers are accustomed to supporting parishioners in a wide range of theological belief. Whether you are a theist, atheist, Christian, humanist, pagan, Deist, nature mystic (the list continues), you find yourself in a category known only to yourself, or you keep changing your mind, the minister will welcome you.

My husband has just been pronounced dead. He's on the couch in the living room. I have no idea what to do.

Your minister will come right over—ministers know about death. They can tell you what your options are; they understand the wide range of emotions you may be feeling and what needs to happen when. Your minister will be your companion during this difficult time.

Crises occur in life—your teenager didn't come home last night, the biopsy was positive, you lost your job, you need to find a nursing home for your father, you didn't mean to get pregnant or you desperately want to, you feel a crushing depression coming on, you feel aimless and empty, your partner is leaving you or you know you need to leave—these are all reasons to call a minister. Ministers are knowledgeable and supportive resources, and they have access to community referrals and congregational connections as well.

I want to have a welcoming ceremony for my new baby.

Our ministers frequently perform rites-of-passage ceremonies: baby dedications, weddings and commitment ceremonies, and funerals or memorial services. Talk with your minister about what the ceremony means to you and what you would like it to look like. Together you can design it.

I like knowing that somebody cares about worship theory, church administration, social justice, pastoral care, ethics, church history, spirituality, world religions, committee dynamics, finance, religious education—you name it.

During the course of their graduate work, our ministers receive training in all of these areas. During their ministerial preparation, in addition to traditional classes in theological school, they may meditate in a Buddhist monastery, teach a curriculum about Jesus to a sixth-grade class, work in a shelter for the homeless, study the Hebrew Bible with the Jesuits, organize fundraising events for a nonprofit agency, revive a moribund membership committee in a local congregation, design a website, manage a suicide hotline, or learn Greek. In addition, in preparation for professional ministry, our clergy must successfully complete internship and chaplaincy programs. Further, they try to live their lives religiously. They have committed themselves to the work of Unitarian Universalism, and they are there to serve you in the context of the religious community.

I want to learn about the long-standing traditions of Unitarian Universalism.

While newcomers to Unitarian Universalism are often impressed by the theological freedom in our congregations, they realize as time goes on that, in spite of the freedom, Unitarian Universalism is a "real" religion, with a distinctive history and culture. Although it is not a dogmatic religion, the newcomer will soon notice common attitudes and practices such as a respect for nature, a desire to seek justice, and a recognition of the worth and dignity of every person. Our ministers talk about, preach about, teach about, and live our particular ways as Unitarian Universalists. How do Unitarian Universalists relate to the world's problems? To whatever may be holy? To children? To those who do not feel empowered? How do we celebrate the holidays? Is this a Christian religion? Jewish? Pagan? Theist? Humanist? In what ways are we spiritual? Heretical? Academic? What are our hymns like? Where do we fit into history? Our ministers stand ready for conversation!

Who Is the Minister?

In the Unitarian Universalist tradition, stereotypes about ministers don't apply:

Stereotype 1: *Ministers dictate what to believe.* In Unitarian Universalism, the minister helps you, the children of the church, and the rest of the congregation develop spirituality, theology, and ways of being religious. Feel free to disagree with the minister! Talk it over!

Stereotype 2: *Ministers fit into a mold.* Unitarian Universalist ministers are people from a wide variety of racial and ethnic heritages. They are old and young and in-between, from every type of economic background. They are gay, straight, bisexual, and transgendered, introverted and extroverted, sophisticated and down-to-earth, hilarious and serious. Our ministers will welcome you, whoever you are.

Stereotype 3: *Ministers judge people.* Our ministers are human, and they understand the human condition. Together, ministers and laypeople work to be the people they would most like to be.

Stereotype 4: *Ministers visit unannounced on Sunday afternoon.* When you want to see a Unitarian Universalist minister, say so! You can find a time and place that works for you— lunch at your office, at home with the baby, a scheduled appointment in the minister's study, at the nursing home, hospital, or prison.

Stereotype 5: *Ministers are the bosses of their congregations.* In Unitarian Universalist churches and fellowships, the members themselves, the laypeople, make democratic decisions. They ordain the minister, they "call" the minister to the church, and, if necessary, they can fire the minister. Members are ultimately responsible for the well-being of the congregation. The minister is not the boss of the congregation.

Ministers and parishioners collaborate to do the work of the church. We do our best to empower one another, whether we are designing a curriculum, planning a social justice event, providing support for a church member in need, scheduling events that foster a sense of religious community, or developing the budget. While professional ministers lend their expertise, Unitarian Universalists honor the "ministries" that each of us offers.

Stereotype 6: *Ministers work for an hour on Sundays and are out of touch with the real world.* The Unitarian Universalist Association credentials ministers who serve the community, ministers who work with children and adults as religious educators, and parish ministers. Most ministers are engaged with the "real world" of people during the day, evenings, and weekends.

During the week, one might find a community minister running a board meeting for an after-school program, writing a press release about the community's response to a homophobic attack, conducting a senior citizens' chorus, or leading a silent retreat. Professional religion educators, in the course of a week, may counsel a child whose grandmother died, facilitate an adult discussion group about sexuality, adapt the preschool Sunday school curriculum, create a worship service, recruit volunteers for the youth group's field trip, and redesign the database for better church school record keeping.

Parish ministers are equally eclectic. Of course they write sermons. But they also meet with the finance committee, the religious education committee, the youth group, the intern committee, the book group, the music committee—the list of meetings is long. They review the budget, write for the newsletter, choose hymns, answer email, meet with parishioners, visit hospitals, help to develop long-range plans, and tend to hundreds of details. Meanwhile, parish ministers also work for social justice in the larger community.

In her poem, "An Observation," May Sarton writes, "Move among the tender with an open hand," and "Stay sensitive up to the end." Ideally, that's what our ministers do.

When things are working well, our ministers love their calling. With all openness and sensitivity, they love the learning, they love the side of goodness, they love the inner spirit, they love the people. In the midst of checking their answering machines, driving like crazy from one appointment to another, coping with the dreaded Saturday night hard disk crash just before someone calls to complain about what's gone awry at an overnight retreat for the youth group—in the midst of the dailiness of their jobs—they move among the tender with an open hand. They cry when their people are in pain, beam with happiness at human triumph, embrace the occasional moment of clarity on a Sunday morning, and have the privilege of working toward justice and mercy, with love.

This is our ministry.

Jane Ranney Rzepka

Our Worship

"O thou beautiful . . . radiance. There is no day nor night, nor form nor color, and never, never a word."

This luminous line from *Gitanjali* was written by Rabindranath Tagore, winner of the 1913 Nobel Prize in literature. Tagore wrote his evocative poems in Bengali and often translated them into English himself. I would like to think that Tagore's religious community, the Brahmo Samaj, which was influenced by nineteenth-century Unitarianism, nourished the spiritual depth of his poetry. The Nobel committee was so taken with the poetry's depth that one member urged his fellows to learn Bengali to better appreciate the original. I find Tagore's poetry, especially his *Gitanjali,* to be a compelling expression of the awe I see at the center of worship.

Awe? The sense of awe that hums in a mother holding her first-born for the first time. The sense of awe that shivers in a young man whose glimpse of the night sky suggests both his significance and his insignificance. The sense of awe echoing in an older woman who suddenly grasps the meaning of her own mortality. The sense of awe that affects true friends in the heat of an honest conversation. The sense of awe that kindles the heart of a man when he watches the morning sun strike his bedroom wall and realizes how glad he is to be alive in that moment, free of past or future.

"Awe" is the word I use to describe what seizes me when I realize that I live at all, that everything *is,* that hope is possible, that limits are to be expected, that tragedy is real, that control is largely an illusion, but that love is nonetheless desirable. "Worship," an ancient and very rich word, well describes my response to that awe: a sense of amazement, a sense of profound gratitude or acceptance, even a bodily trembling. Most often this kind of worship is both solitary and involuntary. I'd guess it is the most common sort of worship in the world, no matter the faith or doubt of the worshipper. Some folks may come to conclusions about God, I suppose, but for the most part, those who know this kind of worship say, with Tagore, "never, never a word."

Worship in Community

Worship has another, more limited meaning, however, that concerns us here. Worship may also describe non-solitary and quite voluntary experiences of artful celebration designed for congregations of *any* Western religious tradition. The Holy Communion at St. John's Lutheran Church, Friday evening Shabbat service over at Temple Beth Shalom, Christmas midnight Mass down at All Saints, and Morning Celebration at Starr King Unitarian Universalist Church are several of the names our spiritual traditions give this other kind of worship. Unitarian Universalists call this time the "service," "Morning Worship," the "Sunday Program," or just plain "worship." Though the content, style, or touchstones of Unitarian Universalist worship will differ from worship in a Friends' Meetinghouse, Greek Orthodox Church,

Reconstructionist Synagogue, or American Buddhist Church, all denominations share the idea of special times, particular ways to structure those times, and the central value of the gathered community. As with every other spiritual group, Unitarian Universalists range in our worship from plain to fancy, from "low church" to "high church," from singular to eclectic. There is no uniform style of worship, no agreed upon pattern of artful celebration among us.

The same is true of setting. Unitarian Universalists gather on Sunday in large rented homes, in striking modern buildings, in whitewashed New England meetinghouses, and in Gothic chapels splashed with the turquoise of stained glass. I know of one congregation that meets in a sort of outdoor amphitheater by the sea and another that meets in a converted barn. In these varied settings, you may find 600 parishioners gathered before a high pulpit or fifteen people sitting on simple wooden chairs in a neon-lit room.

In most of these settings the worship celebration usually lasts for about an hour. On rare evening occasions, such as the ordination of a new minister, the service may take longer. A midweek chapel, on the other hand, might last only thirty minutes. At a celebration like an ordination, you might see robes of rich color and elaborate rituals, such as the laying on of hands. At a regular Sunday celebration, you may see no gowns at all. Very often you will find that leaders of worship wear their finest daily clothes, and you will find the ritual to be relatively spare.

The Order of Worship

Most Unitarian Universalist congregations have an Order of Service, a printed brochure that outlines the structure of celebration as practiced by that particular set of people. Musical preludes or chimes of some sort often begin our services of worship, calling us to attention and initial reflection. Opening words or invocations spoken by a minister or lay leader help us to remember how common worship is connected to our experiences of private awe. Sometimes a choir or the congregation will sing a verse of praise, often called a doxology. Longer hymns or songs of praise to the morning—or to Spirit, to Life, or to Love—are often sung close to the beginning of a service. Also at this point, a fire is often kindled in a wide-brimmed chalice. This ancient symbol of our living tradition reminds us that we are neither the first nor the last persons who so gather. Other congregations light candles "of memory and of hope."

Our children often help to begin our worship celebrations. A story, a skit, a brief homily "to the child in all of us" will sometimes set the tone for the rest of the hour. Sometimes the whole morning is intergenerational.

In the middle of our worship celebrations fall a variety of devotional and community-building activities. Longer silences are sometimes introduced by a bell sound; prayers or meditations from the pulpit (or from the order of service) are sometimes read alone or with the group; image-rich guided meditations are sometimes included in the service. These devotions offer us room to mesh our common, structured experience of worship with the memory of our unstructured, personal experience of awe. In them, we are often invited to remember the whole of our lives, our losses as well as our joys, our desire to grow deeper as well as our desire to be affirmed just as we are. In them, many discern Spirit, named or unnamed.

Recently, some of our congregations have developed rituals around the passages in ordinary human life: the birth of a grandchild, the passing of an exam, the loss of an uncle, the visit of good friends, a divorce or an engagement. Some of these rituals involve lighting candles and telling personal stories; others name loved ones in the middle of a silent meditation. Such rituals of "joys and concerns" may serve to deepen real bonds of community. Some congregations set aside a Sunday each month to memorialize with candles those who have died, a kind of Unitarian Universalist version of the Jewish Kaddish. This openness to grief as well as joy surprises some visitors to our congregations. Although many Unitarian Universalists define worship as a "celebration of Life," a useful phrase coined by Von Ogden Vogt, no one would understand the word "celebration" as lifting up only the happier moments of life. Without a genuine depth and an honest wholeness, group worship can flatten out like foil— shiny, but without weight.

Music as Celebration

After the devotional period in a worship service, choirs may then sing an anthem. From a North American folk tune such as *What Wondrous Love* accompanied on an autoharp to a portion of Leonard Bernstein's exhilarating *Chichester Psalms*, the choral anthem is often a brilliant portion of the service. Moreover, the swell of a great pipe organ resonating a Bach fugue during morning service might well offer the whole meaning of worship to some hearts. String quartets may delight us with Ives, soloists with the jazz style perfected by Odetta. Some of our congregations are developing dance choirs to reinforce the truth that worship is as much an action of the body as a direction of the mind. Several of our smaller congregations get the whole congregation circle-dancing on special Sundays. There is a growing organization, the Unitarian Universalist Musicians' Network, that meets every summer to hone professional skills, exchange ideas, and encourage its members in the musical arts of worship. More and more, music in all its forms reveals itself as a touchstone of Unitarian Universalist worship.

It is rare to experience any worship among us without singing from the congregation. Whether the sound is thin and tentative or echoing off the rafters in four-part harmony, singing remains an essential element in Unitarian Universalist worship. For more than a hundred years, Universalists and Unitarians have enriched not just their own celebrations, but the celebrations of other Western religious traditions as well. Previous Unitarian Universalist hymnbooks, *Hymns of the Spirit* (1937) and *Hymns for the Celebration of Life* (1964), collected congregational songs from many cultures and introduced stunning new texts. Both of these books had wide influence among other religious traditions. The latest Unitarian Universalist hymnbook is called *Singing the Living Tradition* (1993). Spirituals, chants from South Africa, Jewish melodies, Chinese pentatonic tunes, six-part rounds, jazz pieces, and contemporary commissions from Alan Hovhaness and Dede Duson usher us into the wider world that we claim as our common home.

The words sung to these tunes are also revelatory. Originally, Unitarians and Universalists used Christian hymns with references to the Trinity and to hell-fire removed or recast. But for the last hundred years, writers have been experimenting with fresher language in order to move closer to the center of our historic tradition. For example, Unitarian Universalists refer to the Divine in ways often more poetic than doctrinal. "Spirit of Life," "Life of Ages," "Life of Life"— phrases such as these evoke a lively view of the Holy and help us to keep idolatry at bay.

The Power of the Words

The Universalist insistence that salvation is for everyone, not just "the elect," now takes its practical form in the power of language to signify inclusion. Exclusively masculine language in hymns and songs tends to create a world where only men's beliefs, ways, and stories are valued, and fifty percent of the human race becomes invisible. To safeguard the belief in salvation for all people, Unitarians and Universalists have been making the shared language of hymns and songs broader, more reflective of the actual realities of a dual-gender world. Thus, our hymns ought not be seen as artistic additions to the service, but as true expressions of our religious sensibility. They do two amazing things. They express the reality that the earth is indeed inhabited by people of two genders, and they demand greater justice from all who sing of that reality.

There are other concerns, too. We live in a world where beige and brown people are rhetorically called "black" and "white," and where those called "white" claim a centrality denied to those called "black." Hymns that speak of every sin, every diabolical situation as "black" or "dark," and every grace or joy as "white" or "fair" or "of the light" seem to reflect the harmful rhetoric of a divided world. Unitarian Universalists who sing of the beauty of all colors not only receive traditions but also help to remold those traditions to help begin healing the world. It doesn't work like magic, but over time—and with humility of heart—it does work.

The Sermon

Sermons feature so prominently in our worship services that sometimes people talk (albeit inaccurately) as if sermons and worship are synonymous. Good preaching can sometimes threaten to eclipse other parts of a celebration. I've more often wept during sermons than during prayers or rituals. The sermon is often the only time I laugh during an entire service. These are compelling associations. I've also been bored or impatient during sermons. Sermons can be overdone. There have been times after I've preached when I've known at once that the silent meditation was far more meaningful than my confused words.

But a good sermon can provoke a decision that moves a person in a whole new direction. It can lift up a portion of our lives, holding it in just such a light as to reveal facets we couldn't easily see before. A good sermon (and there are many of them) can tug us further down the path toward a difficult forgiveness or remind us of our inestimable value as persons in a world that values little. Sermons can remind us of basic things we've forgotten, help us to learn and unlearn, show us how to reframe the seemingly impossible ideals so that we do not lose hope. I've heard sermons that have helped me question an easy faith, even wrestle with God.

Confessional preaching may invite us to be less tentative about our own truths. Prophetic preaching may rekindle a passion for justice on earth. Good preaching can bring us to the brink of awe no less than the evening star. A sermon may be read from a carefully crafted text or improvised after long mental preparation. It may be memorized or developed from notes. It may be long or short, prosaic or poetic. A sermon can be a dialogue between two people or a story acted out with dramatic props. In any case, the central part of most Unitarian Universalist worship is the sermon, the message, the homily, the talk. A bad sermon may not destroy a worship celebration, but a good sermon certainly enhances one.

Readings are often shared before a sermon, but sometimes they are incorporated into the text of the sermon. These readings may be from just about anywhere. Spiritual readings, from both ancient scripture and more modern sources, are certainly commonplace. But the morning newspaper may feature just as frequently. I also use poems from various cultures and selections from novels or plays. But whether a story from the Gospel of Mark or a poem by Marge Piercy, readings help to root us. They remind us that we neither invented religious liberalism nor do we complete it.

The Variety of Ritual

On certain Sundays you might experience rituals out of our taproot traditions, sacramental or symbolic events of soulful beauty. There may be a "breaking of bread," the ancient ritual of communion inclusively and freshly interpreted. A litany of *Kol Nidrei* may be sung during the Jewish High Holidays. Some of our congregations celebrate the Passover Seder in one form or another, Tenebrae on Good Friday, or the Eucharist on Maundy Thursday. The Flower Communion Festival, a moving ceremony that involves cut flowers, is a common Unitarian Universalist practice held on Easter Sunday or in June. These tangible symbols often prove more significant than either the sermon or the devotions, perhaps because they more effectively address us as whole persons, as bodies and not as mere minds.

Although sermons and rituals often come toward the end of a service, the actual closing of a service usually features a hymn and a blessing or a set of closing words. Often a powerful musical postlude will conclude the celebration.

Some of our congregations do not take up an offering, but the greater number do. The offering, whatever else it may symbolize, is certainly a summons to support the institution that nurtures and encourages liberal thought in religion.

In a Unitarian Universalist congregation, anyone can write a meditation, preach a sermon, or lead a worship celebration. Ordained ministers most often lead worship in our congregations, but lay members have also developed artful skills of celebration. A different quartet of lay members plans worship each week in at least one of our congregations. Most of our congregations seem to have at least one lay-led Sunday per month, when an individual or group plans worship.

Recently, some ministers have started working with a lay associate every Sunday. Guests may be invited: A congresswoman may speak on how her Unitarian Universalist principles guide her decisions, or an astronomer may offer observations on the stars that help elucidate the connection between science and religion. Lest it appear that ordained ministers stick to "spiritual" topics while lay members explore the more secular ideas, I should point out that Thomas Starr King, one of our great nineteenth-century ministers, used to preach brilliant sermons based on such natural phenomena as comets. He even managed to find lessons in the science of metallurgy!

Rites of Passage

Unitarian Universalists join other religious folk in marking the great transitions in a human life—birth, coming-of-age, marriage or union, joining a church, covenanting with a new minister (ordination and installation), death and grieving— each may be celebrated with beauty, poignancy, and depth. It would be helpful to take a closer look at a few of these types of worship.

Marriages for men and women and rites of union for same-sex couples most often occur on weekends at times other than Sunday morning. These are rarely more than a half-hour long and may take a variety of forms, but some public exchange of the couple's consent is usually part of the ceremony.

A memorial or funeral service may involve many people speaking brief remembrances, as well as familiar poems and psalms and direct words about death and grief. These celebrations of peoples' lives vary in length and tone, but I have never left one unmoved.

Unlike weddings or memorial services, the Sunday morning worship most often proves the best setting for the naming of a baby. "Dedication," "naming," or "christening" are the most frequently used terms for such a rite. Godparents may or may not be involved. One common form of such a service involves a rosebud and clear water touched to the child's forehead. Others use water alone, but there is no thought here of a child being born in sin and needing to be washed. "With water, which is as clear as your spirit, my child. . . ." the minister intones. Some ministers use the four elements—earth, air, fire, and water—as blessings on the child's body, intellect, passions, and spirit. The forms are varied, but the joy in such a ceremony is always of a piece.

In *Gitanjali*, Rabindranath Tagore wrote, "The same stream of life that runs through my veins night and day runs through the world and dances in rhythmic measures." Tagore also saw the waves of the sea and every flowering branch or blade of grass as part of that living "stream of life." The stately dance of the seasons, the lifeblood of the body, the breaking forth of the spirit—all of these tributaries flow into a mighty river that summarizes in its perpetual movement the power of worship in the living tradition. Tagore asked, "Is it beyond you to be glad with the gladness of this rhythm?" This question is nothing less than an invitation to leave the superficial behind and to embrace the life of the Spirit.

Mark Belletini

Our Religious Education

The greatest gifts we can give our children, it is said, are "roots and wings." Unitarian Universalist religious education seeks to give us all, no matter what our ages, roots of connection and wings of possibility and hope. Our religious education is lifespan in scope, progressive in theory, experiential in method, and liberal in its theological and ethical perspectives.

The role of liberal religious education toward the end of the twentieth century is to help individuals of all ages experience connections, compassion, and creativity. We need to understand our connection with our liberal religious heritage: the Jewish and Christian roots from which we spring; the Eastern religious traditions that have nurtured us; the insights of philosophy and science that have expanded our knowledge; and our mystical sense of union with one another, our planet, and the universe. We need to feel compassion and act upon it; to empathize with the struggles and joys that are a part of every life journey; to transform oppression into justice; to persevere on behalf of what is right. And finally, we need to encourage and unlock the creativity in each of us in order to utilize fully our individual gifts and, in so doing, to find new solutions to complex problems.

From the Reformation to the Twentieth Century

The roots of liberal religious education go back (as do the roots of liberal religion itself) to the Protestant Reformation. Martin Luther, writing in the sixteenth century, expressed his belief that children are more educable than older people. He showed a basic understanding of the development of the child's cognitive and emotional capacities, and he even suggested the use of games as teaching and learning aids.

In the seventeenth century, John Locke also planted seeds of liberal thinking about religious education. In *Some Thoughts Concerning Education*, published in 1693, Locke critiqued the form of religious education that had developed in the first century following the Reformation. He argued against using the Bible as a primary text for young children, who can have no clear understanding of what it is about.

In the United States, the eighteenth century witnessed a division of thought as to the nature of the child and the type of education needed. The conservative Jonathan Edwards insisted that a child was by nature a hater of God and Goodness and could only become religious by an act of "divine violence" through which the human will was suddenly and miraculously recreated. Charles Chauncy, a liberal, believed that one came to a gradual understanding of religious truths. He did not agree that religious conversion was the only route to individual salvation and offered instead the possibility of growth through religious education.

Although such seeds of liberal religious education were present from the time of the Protestant Reformation, they did not take root for several centuries. The catechism was the educational method of choice for most Catholic and Protestant congregations. With this tool, religious doctrine was put in the form of questions and answers to be memorized by the students. There was no opportunity for the learner to question or explore alternative religious understandings.

The Sunday school movement began in England and the United States in the late eighteenth and early nineteenth centuries as an attempt to offer secular schooling to children who worked in factories the other six days of the week. Congregational churches in New England formed such schools and soon added the teaching of morals and religion to the curriculum. Some of these congregations became officially Unitarian in the early part of the nineteenth century. Universalist Sunday schools had their beginnings in Philadelphia in 1790, when Dr. Benjamin Rush helped found the "First Day" or "Sunday School Society."

In 1833, Henry Ware, Jr., made the first attempt to produce a curriculum for the Unitarian Sunday schools in the form of a series of books about the life and times of Jesus and the history of Christianity. In 1837, ten years after the formation of the Boston Sunday School Society (later to become the Unitarian Sunday School Society), the Reverend William Ellery Channing was asked to give the main address at the annual meeting. In his travels to England, Channing had become aware of more liberal approaches to education, and in his address he offered his co-religionists in Boston some truly revolutionary ideas. He declared that the Sunday school movement should be responsive to the needs and capacities of children. His eloquent words are still quoted today in many Unitarian Universalist religious education materials:

> The great end in religious instruction . . . is not to stamp our minds irresistibly on the young but to stir up their own; not to make them see with our eyes but

to look inquiringly and steadily with their own; not
to give them a definite amount of knowledge but to
inspire a fervent love of truth; not to form an outward
regularity but to touch inward springs. . . .

Unfortunately, Channing's vision was not put into actual
practice for almost seventy-five years, until the "New Beacon
Course in Religious Education" was created by the American
Unitarian Association shortly after the turn of the twentieth
century.

Process and Method

Liberal religious education in this century has focused as
much on process and method as it has on content. Perhaps the
two most prominent pioneers in this effort were Sophia Lyon
Fahs, a Unitarian religious educator, and Angus MacLean, a
Universalist minister and professor at St. Lawrence Theological School in Canton, New York.

Fahs came to Unitarianism from a Presbyterian family background. While working for a Master of Arts degree at the Teachers College of Columbia University in New York, she became
involved in the experimental Sunday school at the College,
which was based on progressive principles of education,
particularly the work of John Dewey. It was here that she began
to develop and articulate her vision for religious education.

Fahs believed in a naturalistic theism that utilized scientific knowledge and empirical process to understand and
appreciate the mysteries of life. Her goal was to change "the
conception of the educational process from one of indoctrina-
tion and acceptance of authority to one of creative discovery,
intelligent examination, and free decision."

In 1931, she was asked to join a committee that was
studying the curricula of the American Unitarian Association

(AUA). As a result of that experience, she was offered a position at the AUA as curriculum editor working with Ernest Kuebler, the new Secretary of the Department of Religious Education. Kuebler and Fahs instituted a new era, not only in Unitarian religious education, but in liberal religious education in general. The New Beacon Series they produced is still regarded as a milestone in the field. This curriculum is based on the principle that religious educators can facilitate a person's spiritual growth through interaction with carefully chosen materials and with the environment. It is not a "course of study" but more a guide to assist teachers and learners to grow together into an awareness of the spiritual meaning of living. Self-esteem, appreciation of others' values and experiences, and shaping the person into a psychologically well-adjusted, emotionally healthy, socially conscious person are some of its progressive aims.

A very important Universalist who influenced liberal religious education during this time was Angus MacLean. MacLean was a professor of religious education at the Theological School of St. Lawrence University. He contributed to the atmosphere out of which the New Beacon Series arose.

For MacLean, "A religion that seeks to serve the living generation is the only one that can fully embrace all time." Past experience has value only in terms of present purpose. Education for MacLean was the process of continuous and creative sharing in the life of humankind. He believed that church school teachers needed to bring "more of the child's normal life into the school, more of [his or her] natural concerns and interests and more of the things to which the child's purpose and interest most easily attach themselves."

The process and methods used today continue to focus on materials appropriate to the developmental stage of the learner. There are stories and resources from a variety of religious and secular traditions. There are activities to help make the learning come alive—from arts and crafts to music, drama, and dance. Learners are encouraged to question, to pull and tug at difficult problems and dilemmas. Different backgrounds, beliefs, and viewpoints are celebrated. There is also an invitation to share the vision and values articulated in our Unitarian Universalist Principles and Purposes. There is an attempt made to acknowledge and utilize a variety of learning styles in order that students feel affirmed, not inadequate. Teachers are encouraged to model a continuing search for greater understanding. There is awareness of the reality that religious education is truly a lifelong process. What then do this process and method offer to those who have chosen Unitarian Universalism as their religious path?

Connections

One of the most important things Unitarian Universalist religious education tries to offer its students of all ages is a sense of connection. This connection begins in infancy as the newborn child feels its bond to parents and family. The congregation's welcoming of the infant into a warm and inviting nursery atmosphere and its affirmation of the worth of each child in the Child Welcoming, or Dedication, Ceremony are ways of enlarging this bond from family to religious community. Programs for young children focus on strengthening feelings of self-worth and self-esteem as these youngsters start making friends outside the home. Introductions to our Unitarian Universalist congregations are handled with care and creative techniques. Intergenerational events where people of all ages play and learn together are especially important and create a sense of connection with the entire religious community.

As the young child enters elementary school and progresses through the years of schooling toward high school, connections to other faiths are made—connections to our Jewish and Christian roots as well as to other world religions. How Unitarian Universalists utilize philosophy, the scientific method, and other intellectual traditions is also an important "religious" connection made in our curricula.

Our youth organization, Young Religious Unitarian Universalists (YRUU), serves youth from ages fourteen to twenty. YRUU utilizes both curriculum materials as well as the interests of the teens themselves to determine the agenda for youth group meetings. In conjunction with their adult advisors, youth groups plan a variety of programs. These programs take on many forms from sessions on spirituality and religion, to hands-on experiences with social justice projects, to parties for fun and fellowship. Regional, district, and continental youth conferences offer our teenagers yet another way to connect with one another and with our larger movement.

The role of parents in religious education is critical. The hour of church school once a week is only a small window of opportunity in which to encourage religious growth. The real religious education takes place in the home, as children and youth observe how their elders live out their values and beliefs.

Adult education materials help adults—who may be new to the denomination or longtime Unitarian Universalists—grapple with defining their own beliefs. This is an integral part of the liberal religious enterprise. Many of our congregations are developing exciting local adult programming, which includes courses on world religions, liberal theology, Unitarian Universalist history, and topics of current ethical concern.

In our approach to religious education, we utilize the best understandings of human development—cognitive, emotional, and religious. We explore how new findings about the human brain can help break down old blocks of prejudice. We reach for new techniques in learning theory and holistic education to help all individuals strengthen their sense of bondedness with the universe. We value our connections with one another and the world because it is through such connections that we are invited into compassion.

Compassion

Throughout our liberal religious history, we have been blessed with women and men whose compassion and courage provide examples for us all. We learn about heroines and heroes such as Dorothea Dix, Clara Barton, Horace Mann, and James Reeb in our lifespan religious education classes. We recognize that their struggles are with us today in different forms. We are reminded by their work that, if we do not feel compassion, we may well stunt our lives and threaten the future of our planet.

In all of our religious education programming—be it church school, youth groups, intergenerational events, or adult education—we offer as a ground rule for all our activities the acceptance of one another and the valuing of our inherent worth and dignity as persons. We acknowledge that there is evil, pain, and suffering in the world. We do not close our eyes to any of this. We commit ourselves to trying to understand how to help individuals and groups untie knots of pain and anger. We commit ourselves to stand with one another through the joys and sorrows that affect every life.

We often encourage our church school classes to include social action as part of their educational processes. One seventh- and eighth-grade class in a Philadelphia congregation focused its efforts on the need to care for the earth by recycling paper. The students learned about church governance when they convinced the board of the church to vote in favor of a recycling proposal that called for the use of more white than colored paper in any printing done by the church. They persuaded the adults to put out bins so that parishioners could recycle their Sunday programs when they were finished with them.

In our religious education programs, we also try to find ways to support and encourage the work of many heroic individuals in our congregations who quietly go about the hard work of trying to make the world a better place every day. When a church member in Virginia retired from his lifetime work as the owner and chief chef of a diner, for example, he began working five days a week as the breakfast cook for a local homeless program. He still rose at 4 A.M., but his destination was very different. I remember the response of the church school children who heard him tell his story. He was not boasting. He was glad to be of help and merely shared in honesty the challenges he faced in serving the homeless. In the next few weeks, the children mounted a drive to bring to the congregation's attention the need for more food for the shelter. The result was an outpouring of gifts, a testament to "compassion"—that is, passion with and for the struggles of others.

Offering compassion is difficult when there are as many demands upon us as there are today. Our religious education programs engage us in the act of compassion: the offering of a helping hand, walking together for a cause, the solidarity felt in a community social action project. It is such engagement that can rekindle our spirits in important ways. And it is this spirit that inspires the third component of liberal religious education: creativity.

Creativity

With William Ellery Channing's call to us in 1837 to "touch inward springs," the seed of creativity was planted in the ground of liberal religious education. It took decades before it bore fruit. And yet, with each evolutionary turn of Unitarian and Universalist religious education, more and more emphasis has been placed on this important foundation of the liberal religious quest. Gabriel Moran, a noted liberal religious educator, expresses it eloquently when he says that "religious education is the attempt to keep education open to the undreamt-of possibilities of the human race."

I am very aware of the changes that take place as our children move from the wide-eyed, wonderful imagination of young childhood into a more closed and limited mode of engagement with the world, as schools and society try to define for us what is and what is not real, actual, or possible. Our Unitarian Universalist religious education programs are places where dreams may be kindled or rekindled, where wondering and imagination can be affirmed, where new talents can be tried in safe settings. An adult class in religious dance, a course in poetry writing, a workshop in art for the non-artistic can open doors for people, no matter what their ages. Intergenerational events in which all ages try their talents at something new are especially rich times for growth. Non-competitive games can open doors to new fun for those who have not felt especially gifted athletically. An afternoon kite-making and kite-flying event can help spirits soar.

The challenges facing each of us can best be met when our creative potential is open and flowing. The more affirmed a person feels in using her or his own individual creative gifts, the more likely she or he will be able to handle a situation with a sense of connection, compassion, and maturity. The more frustrated the inner flame of being, the more likely a person is to respond in blocked, prejudiced, and limited ways.

Connections, compassion, and creativity are the gifts of lifespan liberal religious education. Ours is a tradition that has long nurtured such values. Ours is a tradition that is open to continuing growth and new learnings in these areas. Ours is a tradition that invites every individual to be an integral part of the creation of such religious education programs, activities, and events. In such ways, we further our vision of a responsive and responsible religious community.

Makanah Elizabeth Morriss

Our Work for Social Justice and Diversity

Working for justice in our world is a principle way for Unitarian Universalists to express faith. Many people undertake social justice work to show their gratitude for life's gifts and their commitment to making our world the best place for all. Depending on their theologies—Jewish, Humanistic, earth-centered, Jesus-centered, Buddhist—individual Unitarian Universalists have different ways of verbalizing their motivations. However, the preciousness of life on earth, as opposed to future life in a far-away paradise, and the inherent worth and dignity of every person with whom we share the planet, emerge as common themes for undertaking social justice work.

Throughout Unitarian and Universalist history, women and men have shown great courage and taken huge personal risks on behalf of their visions of a more just and equitable society. Famous American Unitarians and Universalists such as suffragist Susan B. Anthony, civil rights leader Whitney Young, diplomat Adlai Stevenson, or American Red Cross founder Clara Barton, are far outnumbered by the literally hundreds and thousands of Unitarian Universalists who have spent decades laboring for justice in their own communities. Many Unitarian Universalists work professionally in service fields as teachers, health professionals, therapists, social workers, and government workers. Many leaders in secular justice-making organizations such as the American Civil Liberties Union, Planned Parenthood, the National Association for the Advancement of Colored People, the Sierra Club, and Common Cause, are also Unitarian Universalists. Still others work in interfaith coalitions or in specifically Unitarian Universalist organizations for justice. We aren't a large religious body, but we are mighty!

In 1995, when UUA Moderator Denise Davidoff was invited for the first time to the White House, she was astonished that the people there knew so much about the Unitarian Universalist Association. White House officials thanked her for the cutting-edge work of Unitarian Universalists around the United States, particularly in organizing interfaith responses to the religious right. That Unitarian Universalists have made an impression was similarly indicated at the 1998 Road to Victory Conference, a major gathering of religious right groups, held annually in Washington, DC, by Pat Robertson's Christian Coalition. In a workshop on interfaith organizing, presented at that conference, the Christian Coalition's field director was asked to give tips about how to get clergy on board with Christian Coalition enterprises. "I'll give you a tip," he responded, "Don't start with the Unitarian Universalists!"

Freedom of religion has been one of our central themes since the Unitarian Universalist Association came into existence. Unitarians in particular were key actors in the 1950s in the movement to outlaw prayer in public schools. As we move into the twenty-first century, Unitarian Universalists remain extremely active in defending religious freedom in the United States and all over the world. For over thirty years, we have also stood firm on a woman's right to choose abortion and the worth and dignity of non-heterosexual members of society.

The members of the Unitarian Universalist Association do not always agree on what constitutes a worthy cause, or on how to express our support or opposition to various initiatives. Our belief in congregational polity means that any congregation has the right to support the issues it desires. Some congregations do not want to take any stands at all. Unitarian Universalist congregations encourage individuals to speak for themselves, but never in the name of the congregation. At our annual General Assemblies, where delegates from member congregations vote on Association business, statements of conscience are passed that reflect the will of the gathered voting body. These statements become the basis of reference for anyone speaking on behalf of the UUA.

UUA President John Buehrens has referred to our congregations on numerous occasions as "training centers for democracy." He means that each of our congregations is democratically structured and governed, and that at our best we learn kindness and responsibility, which can help us to create a more just democratic society at large. Some of our most effective social justice programs started from an individual members' heart, soul, or mind, before moving into a congregation's life, mission, and purpose, and then ultimately into the wider society.

This progression is true of most of our efforts to combat oppressions, both in society and in our religious community. In 1997, the Unitarian Universalist Association created the Faith in Action Department to help link all the anti-oppression efforts in our movement. The department's mission is to transform Unitarian Universalism into an anti-oppression, multicultural religious community that affirms the inherent worth and dignity of every person. By collaborating with

Unitarian Universalists in congregations, districts, seminaries, and associate and affiliate groups, we develop new relationships in our communities and we learn to initiate and restructure our justice efforts to be more effective, authentic, and accountable to oppressed communities. The following outline examines key issues of oppression that Unitarian Universalists are working to overcome.

Bisexual, Gay, Lesbian, and Transgender Concerns

In 1970 the UUA General Assembly passed a resolution to end discrimination against homosexuals and bisexuals and called on congregations to develop sex education programs that promote healthy attitudes toward all forms of sexuality. Since that time Unitarian Universalists have developed curricula designed to counter homophobia and teach a more positive attitude toward gay, lesbian, and bisexual people. In 1975 the UUA General Assembly voted to fund an Office of Gay Affairs that would be staffed by gay people and serve as a resource to members of the UUA.

Subsequent General Assembly resolutions have urged the Association and the Unitarian Universalist Minister's Association to assist in settling openly gay and lesbian ministers with churches, affirmed those ministers who provide services of union to lesbian and gay couples, and urged Unitarian Universalists to work to end AIDS discrimination through education and advocacy.

A 1989 General Assembly resolution called for the creation of the Welcoming Congregation program, which is designed to ensure that congregations welcome gay, lesbian, bisexual, and transgender people. Since the inception of that program, 40 percent of our congregations have now declared themselves to be officially "welcoming." Following the internal examination and commitment that is entailed in such a program, many welcoming congregations have become actively involved in promoting legislation that supports gay, lesbian, bisexual, and transgender people, or in providing services to non-heterosexual youth, or in fighting homophobic initiatives of the religious right.

Racial Justice

Unitarian Universalists have called for racial justice ever since the first UUA General Assembly in 1961. Many Unitarian Universalists have been deeply involved in the civil rights struggles of the twentieth century, working toward racial assimilation and integration. However, it is not enough to address the emerging demands for empowerment of people of color. We did not know then what Unitarian Universalist professor of religion and Black studies Dr. William Jones teaches us today—that working for assimilation without first creating equality simply perpetuates inequality.

The debates in the mid-1960s about integration vs. empowerment of people of color were so heated that they led some, both whites and people of color, to leave the Unitarian Universalist Association. It took the Unitarian Universalist movement over a decade to begin to heal the wounds from the empowerment controversy—to acknowledge our mistakes, renew our commitment, and sharpen our understanding about the new face of racism that began to emerge in the 1980s.

Historically, individual Unitarians and Universalists have been on the cutting edge of social justice advocacy, but the Association itself has been ill-prepared to recognize and acknowledge institutional racism within Unitarian Universalism. Much of our inaction and ambivalence can be traced to some of our institutional characteristics: the emphasis on individual belief as opposed to corporate credos, the emphasis on freedom of conscience as opposed to freedom from oppression, and our widely touted tolerance for the opinions of others, coupled with our failure to understand the need for tolerance with equality.

In 1981, recognizing that racism had not gone away and had in fact, become insidiously worse throughout society, the Unitarian Universalist Association commissioned an Institutional Racism Audit that evaluated questions of racial equity in hiring practices and policy at UUA headquarters. The Board of Trustees adopted the following anti-racism imperative in 1981 and reaffirmed it in 1989.

> Recognizing the fact that institutional racism is still embedded in American society in 1981, the Unitarian Universalist Association shall seek to eliminate racism in all its institutional structures, policies, practices, and patterns of behavior so that it will become a racially equitable institution and can make an effective contribution toward achieving a similarly equitable society.

Knowing that words alone were not enough, a series of task forces for monitoring racism was subsequently established. The UUA helped establish several intentionally multiracial congregations with people of color as the founding ministers.

An intentional effort was launched to racially diversify staff at UUA headquarters and an affirmative action officer was appointed. A new staff position at the UUA was created in 1987 to focus on racial and urban concerns. In 1989, the Office of Racial Inclusiveness was established.

A series of meetings from 1990 to 1992 among grassroots committees, affinity groups, the UUA administration, UUA staff, and the Board of Trustees laid the groundwork for developing a long-range initiative for racial and cultural diversity.

At the 1992 General Assembly, a resolution titled "Racial and Cultural Diversity in Unitarian Universalism" was passed. The significance of this experience is captured by the Reverend Victor Carpenter, the maker of the motion:

> We have been provided with that rarest of human opportunities—a second chance. Twenty-five years ago we had the opportunity to lead this country's religious community in the direction of racial justice. We rose up and we fell back. The vision was too blurred, the rhetoric too harsh, the pain too deep. Now we are again given a chance to lead this nation in generous response to the social crisis symbolized by [the] Los Angeles [civil disturbances]. We are called to do justly, to love mercy, and to work humbly for the empowerment of our brothers and sisters. Let's not blow it.

This time we didn't blow it. In fact we did something rare for Unitarian Universalists; we passed the resolution unanimously.

Beginning with the creation in 1988 of the African American Unitarian Universalist Ministries (AAUUM), several continental organizations have been formed to nurture and support people of color. AAUUM was formed as a continental organization for African-American ministers and religious professionals. In 1995 the Latino/a Unitarian Universalist Networking Association (LUUNA) was created to nurture and support Latino/a Unitarian Universalists and to further understanding of Latino/a issues within Unitarian Universalism. In 1997, the Diverse and Revolutionary Unitarian Universalist Multicultural Ministry (DRUUMM) was formed to support and nurture Unitarian Universalist religious professionals of color.

The 1997 General Assembly passed a resolution that called on the UUA to work toward becoming an anti-racist, anti-oppressive, multicultural religious community. The vision statement for this initiative, named "Journey Toward Wholeness," states:

> An authentically anti-oppressive, anti-racist Unitarian Universalist faith will be an equitable, proactive, soul-transforming, prophetic force for justice within our congregations and communities. This faith will be effective and accountable, both to itself and to our communities, through transformative spirituality, justice seeking, witness, and action.

The Journey Toward Wholeness initiative is a process that assists Unitarian Universalist congregations and organizations to correctly identify their own levels of diversity and anti-racism and to move to increase both. Participation in the journey provides our congregations and organizations with resources, curricula, programs, training, and consultation for moving through six stages of institutional practice and awareness ranging from monocultural exclusive to anti-racist multicultural.

To become an anti-racist multicultural institution requires commitment, analysis, strategy, resources, and a willingness to risk, grow, and change. This deeply relational work can move all of us closer to the wholeness we yearn for.

Ableism and Accessibilities

Ableism is yet another issue in which Unitarian Universalists are called by our faith to seek justice and break the barriers that exist in society at large, in our congregations, and in ourselves.

General Assembly resolutions in 1977 urged our congregations to study and implement methods for integrating people with special needs into both our own and the larger society. In 1993, recognizing that people with disabilities are often excluded from our religious community because of barriers created by architecture, attitude, and communication, a Task Force on Accessibilities was appointed to review the accessibility needs of our congregations and association and to make recommendations for resources and actions.

The Task Force urged the UUA to commit itself to "removing all barriers—attitudinal, physical, and programmatic—that prevent people with disabilities from fully participating in the life of our association." It also recommended that staff time and attention be given to this work. To provide strategic planning, implementation, oversight, and support to our congregations, the UUA Board of Trustees appointed an Accessibilities Committee.

The basis for our anti-oppression work is a trusting community in which mistakes may be made without blame or judgment, in which individuals are free to draw their own conclusions and to listen to their own consciences, and in which the love of community will not be lost because of differing opinions. This is always a struggle, and this is why our congregations are great places to learn about living in a democratic society.

The focus for Unitarian Universalists in the twenty-first century will most likely be on economic justice issues. As a movement primarily composed of people from middle- and upper middle-class backgrounds, the struggle for accountability and clear conscience around economic issues will make confronting the privileges of white skin or heterosexual orientation look like a piece of cake! It is important, therefore, that our communities stay strong and function well, because we need each other to do this difficult but critical work.

As we work to ensure that our communities include people of all ages, physical abilities, races, financial circumstances, sexual orientations, national origins, educational backgrounds, and spiritual understandings, we will learn how to create the Beloved Community of which we all dream. In such communities, the gifts of all are valued and needed, whether parent or artist, bookkeeper or bus driver. This, indeed, is the training ground for living in democracy!

If you have a passion for a particular justice issue, the likelihood is good that there is a Unitarian Universalist group that would love to have you as a member. Unitarian Universalists have formed in small organizations to stop the death penalty, confront violence against women, promote stewardship of our planet, promote economic justice, fight heterosexism, preserve religious liberty, and do just about anything else you can imagine! Browse through the back of the UUA Directory, available in every congregation, to learn how to get in touch with any of these organizations.

In addition, the Unitarian Universalist Service Committee (UUSC), an independent member organization committed to human rights domestically and abroad, has developed a number of summer work camps, for adults and youth, that engage Unitarian Universalists in activities from rebuilding burned churches to organizing for labor rights. Contact the Unitarian Universalist Service Committee at 130 Prospect Street, Cambridge, Massachusetts 02139.

Jacqui James and Meg Riley

Sharing Our Faith:
Two Perspectives

William Sinkford:

I found Unitarian Universalism after experiencing other faith communities in my search for a religious home.

I walked into my first Unitarian Universalist congregation at the age of fourteen, almost forty years ago. To say that I had been searching for a religious home would give me far more credit than I deserve. The reality was that I had been accompanying my mother as she searched for a religious home for both of us. And I must acknowledge that I was not always enthusiastic about this search. Churches hadn't been very comfortable places for me, let alone supportive religious homes.

My nuclear family had been unchurched throughout my early years. We are African-American and had attended the Black Episcopal Church in Detroit, Michigan, and the Black Southern Baptist Church in North Carolina. Even at fourteen, I knew that I did not fit in either church.

The Black Southern Baptist Church in the small North Carolina town where my mother had been reared was the life of the Black community. Everyone knew they were welcome there. But in addition to this sense of acceptance and the joyful song and prayer life, "hell-fire" was preached from the pulpit. Somehow I could not believe in a God who would damn some people to hell.

The Black Episcopal Church in Detroit was light on hell-fire, but heavy on the liturgical mysteries of transubstantiation and the strange concept (to me) of the triune God. This upper middle-class congregation seemed far more concerned with the labels in my clothes and the type of car we drove than with the state of my soul, let alone with my theological struggles.

By age fourteen I had decided that Christianity was not for me. As I look back, I understand that my age at the time was at least as important as my theological journey. I took considerable pleasure in the consternation of family and friends when I proclaimed a "stand-up" atheism, savoring the predictable shocked reaction and welcoming the debate that was sure to follow.

My family tried a Bahii community and several other mainline Protestant churches, but it was not until we walked into First Unitarian in Cincinnati, Ohio, that I found my religious home. Most of the faces in the congregation were white, but many African Americans also were present. The congregation had been very active in the struggle to dismantle segregation in that border town, and African Americans had been drawn to the church and welcomed as members. The religious educator, Pauline Warfield Lewis, who guided me to the youth group that night, was African-American. I didn't take any polls of course; I don't know if 10 percent or 20 percent of the congregation were Black, but there were enough persons of color that I knew it was okay to be Black and to be in the presence of whites.

No hell-fire was preached from the pulpit. A personal search for meaning and a commitment to justice were the messages. Even my aggressive atheism was acceptable. Not everyone I talked to agreed with me—far from it—but people wanted to hear what was in my heart. I was engaged less in debate and more in conversation in which sharing was possible, perhaps even expected.

I felt wanted and valued by this congregation. "Would you like to join the youth group?" "We're hosting a conference this weekend, can you come?" "Would you help with a worship service?" This was a place where I could bring my whole person.

As a minister now, I sometimes interpret my experience in theological terms: The inherent worth and dignity of every person. Commitment to justice, equity, and compassion. The value of personal story as the basis for theological reflection and religious life. The need to make our congregations places where people do not need to check their identities at the door. The extraordinary experience of covenanted community committed to living out religious values in the world.

But the reality of my experience has been both less lofty and more profound. The First Unitarian Church in Cincinnati truly welcomed me. The members of the congregation offered themselves in ways that gave me the gift of myself. The standard they embodied was not merely tolerance, but affirmation. I hope and trust that you have had a similar experience in finding your Unitarian Universalist congregation. This faith can be your home.

Since age fourteen, I have had many opportunities to talk about Unitarian Universalism. I have talked to people looking for a new church home and people who have recently moved and become my neighbors. I have chatted with other parents on the sidelines of soccer games or swim meets, sharing bits of personal or family stress. Sometimes in social gatherings it's gratifying to talk about my church and to hear friends say how important the church sounds in my life.

But sometimes, as if by an act of grace, a conversation will happen, not at my bidding, where the good news of Unitarian Universalism offers hope to someone in need. A few years ago I was riding with another minister in a cab in New York City, on the way to a meeting at one of our congregations. The driver was a recent Haitian immigrant who was, I think, practicing his American English on his passengers.

"What is your business?" he asked. After we told him we were Unitarian Universalist ministers, he asked how our church felt about gay and lesbian people. We answered with our clear affirmation that all people are children of God, that gay and lesbian folks are welcomed in our congregations and in our ministry.

The cabby was silent for a moment and then told the story of his brother, a gay man who had been forced out of his religious home when he was outed in his congregation. "Unitarian Universalist, you say? I wonder if he has heard about your church. I'm glad I have. We need to find a church where we can be together as a family."

I don't know whether this man and his family sought out a Unitarian Universalist congregation. We did suggest a few for him to visit, but I do believe that he just needed to know there was at least one church where his family could be together as who they really are.

Our Unitarian Universalist tradition and worshipping communities can help people heal their wounds, build their confidence, find opportunities for self-forgiveness, and restore their self-worth. We need never fear the value of what we have to offer. May you find your religious home as I have.

Kay Montgomery:

I invented Unitarian Universalism. All by myself. I know numerous other people who have done this as well. I did it on buses, traveling up and down Livernois Avenue in Detroit. I was seventeen or so, a working-class Irish Catholic, living with my parents and attending a Jesuit college about ten miles away. The Jesuits would have been astonished, I suppose, to learn that this is what they had fashioned: a teenager trying to figure out what religion was and could be, and whether it was even possible to be both religious and honest much less an actual member of an actual church. I thought not. Each day that bus went within a half-mile or so of a Unitarian church, but I didn't know that and, if I had known, it wouldn't have meant a thing.

A decade later in another city, long after I had left "The Church," I stumbled on a passage in a book that described Unitarian Universalism. I was astonished: This thing I had invented actually existed—a richer version than mine, a version with a religious, intellectual, and cultural tradition I couldn't have imagined, but still, identifiably mine. And then there was the experience so many of us have had—of coming home. Of showing up in this church and finding comfort and challenge and people who insisted that I grow, of finding ideas that thrilled and scared me because they demanded so much, of finding a community of scrappy, smart, satisfying people who cared passionately about the church, about Unitarian Universalism, and about leaving the planet a better place, people who believe that they need one another for religious and social reasons, and for the work of making justice.

Unitarian Universalists come from so many places: parents who want their children to be religious but not limited by creeds; community activists who want a religious grounding for their work; people who left a traditional religion because they grew uncomfortable with its message; those with generations of Unitarian or Universalist forebears; gay, lesbian, bisexual, and/or transgendered people who want a church where they will feel welcomed and where their partnerships will be blessed; bi-racial families; couples from different faiths who join because they want to be married by a clergyperson who will respect and honor their traditions and then decide to stay. Many paths are traveled on the way to Unitarian Universalism.

But what about the folks who don't even know this faith exists, who have some sense of what they wish existed but can't imagine that it does? The kids or young adults or retired men and women on a bus somewhere in some city, longing for something that could be right around the corner or down a street from where they are. What about those people? How does Unitarian Universalism reach them?

Unitarian Universalist churches often exist as small (or sometimes medium-sized or even largish) enclaves of "the chosen." An unspoken feeling seems to exist that if you're smart enough to find us, we'll let you in. Signage is sometimes poor, advertising is non-existent, and many of us hesitate to invite others to join us at church on Sunday for fear of proselytizing in a way that is disrespectful or pushy. And often we feel inadequate about finding the right words to describe our faith—as though we might fail an exam.

A few years ago I had an experience that changed my feelings about inviting others into my own, chosen, faith tradition. My brother was dying, the sibling I had always been closest to. For months I spent as many weekends as I could traveling from Boston to Detroit. Those weeks were fraught with pain and grief, but also with unexpected moments of something like joy. John and I and the rest of the family cried and laughed together, and odd and amazing things happened, because in the midst of this tragedy, this watching of a marathon runner curled on his bed like a child, there was space only for honesty.

Odd and amazing things happened, but none more odd and amazing than this: Johnny experienced a deathbed conversion. My Roman Catholic brother became a Unitarian Universalist.

He gathered us, his wife, his grown sons, and me, and asked that a friend of mine, the Reverend Terasa Cooley, then minister of the First Unitarian Universalist Church in Detroit (yes, the very church I had passed decades earlier), be asked to minister to him for his last few weeks and days. The memorial service was held in that church, attended by hundreds of people who couldn't sing the hymns. I smiled, honored to have witnessed this final act of integrity, and pleased to know that he and I were more alike than we had guessed. I was also sad that his life—so rich in most ways—had not been as religiously satisfying as his death. And conscious that the one person who might have changed that was . . . me. I had talked about Unitarian Universalism of course—it is central to my life—but the one thing I hadn't done, hadn't even thought of doing, was urge him to join me there.

This is what I have learned: For each time I don't reach out to someone who might join this faith, for each time I hesitate to be hospitable, out of shyness or solipsism, I may be leaving someone's life poorer than it might be. If there's a teenager on a bus somewhere—and there is—I'd like to offer her the good news of Unitarian Universalism.

William Sinkford and Kay Montgomery

Our Roots

The Unitarian Universalist Association is of recent origin. It came into being in Boston, Massachusetts, in 1961, with the consolidation of the American Unitarian Association and the Universalist Church of America. Although Unitarians and Universalists had separate organizational histories in the United States, their antecedents are intertwined in past culture and religions. So it is that the Unitarian Universalist Association and the more than 1,000 churches and fellowships that form its constituency have common roots that run to the distant past.

Origins of Our Faith

Universalism has taken on different meanings at different times. There is an important element of truth in this comment by Universalist minister L. B. Fisher: "Universalists are often asked to tell where they stand. The only true answer to give to this question is that we do not stand at all, we move." In 1791, the Universalist Benjamin Rush, a physician and a signer of the Declaration of Independence, described Universalism as "a belief in God's universal love to all His creatures." He went on to say that God "will finally restore all of them who are miserable to happiness."

Taken by itself, this was a remarkable statement in an age when belief in eternal hell-fire and damnation was common. But Rush went further and declared that the belief in God's universal love "leads to truths upon all subjects, more especially upon the subject of government. It establishes the *equality* of mankind [sic]—it abolishes the punishment of death for any crime and converts jails into houses of repentance and reformation." Rush encouraged American Universalists gathered in Philadelphia in 1790 to adopt these advanced principles as well as a far-reaching declaration stating that "although defensive wars are lawful, there is a time coming when universal love . . . will put an end to all wars." That early Universalists saw social action growing inevitably out of theological belief should not be lost on us.

Scholars trace Universalism back to the Alexandrian Christian School of the early church fathers, Clement and Origen of the third century. The roots go back even farther—to the universal inclusiveness of Jesus' gospel message, the teachings of Buddha and Confucius, as well as Greek Orphic religion and the Ionian philosophers who taught about universals and a unified lawful cosmos. The Universalist teaching that the whole human race will be "saved," embodied in Jesus' teachings, was condemned as a heresy by a church council in 544 CE.

Unitarianism shares this common origin in the early Greek faith in the unity of all existence, as well as the belief of the early Jewish Christians in the human prophet Jesus as the Messiah or Son of Man, ushering in the new reign of heaven. The first official use of the Unitarian name, however, occurred in 1600 in Transylvania, a province of the Austro-Hungarian Empire that only became part of Romania after

World War I. At that moment in history, "Unitarian" referred to those who believed in the toleration of other faiths and the unity of God (as opposed to the doctrine of the Trinity). Hence the meanings of the word Unitarian go back to theological controversies about Jesus that the church attempted to settle by a decision about the Trinity—that the Father, Son, and Holy Spirit are the same substance in three persons, promulgated at the famous Council of Nicaea in 325 CE.

Other chapters in this *Pocket Guide* deal with contemporary meanings of "Unitarianism" and "Universalism." But we note that the meanings have never stood still for long. It has been central to our tradition to understand truth as an evolving, growing reality and to understand that no one person, church, science, or generation can grasp the whole of truth or define it once and for all.

Our churches have existed and our beliefs have been foreshadowed in different places and at different times. Michael Servetus was perhaps the earliest of the Reformation anti-Trinitarians. He bore the unique distinction of being burned in effigy by the Roman Catholics and in actuality by the Protestant-Calvinists. He was burned at the stake in Geneva in 1553 with his great theological opus, *The Restitution of Christianity*, tied to his thigh.

In his book *Hunted Heretic*, Roland Bainton writes that Servetus

> brought together in a single person the Renaissance and the left wing of the Reformation. He was at once a disciple of the Neoplatonic Academy at Florence and of the Anabaptists. The scope of his interests and accomplishments exhibits . . . the 'universal man' of the Renaissance, for Servetus was proficient in medicine, geography, biblical scholarship, and theology.

In him, the most diverse tendencies of the Renaissance and the Reformation were blended.

Clearly, he was among the most radical theologians who
stressed the union of the human and divine, and put forward
the universalistic ideal of the unity of the dominant faiths of
his time—Christianity, Judaism, and Islam.

Our connections with the Renaissance have been under-
scored also by the Unitarian Universalist historian Arnold
Crompton, who, in an earlier edition of this *Pocket Guide*, wrote:

Under the still powerful influence of the Renaissance,
scholar preachers in the university towns of Florence,
Bologna, and Padua practiced complete freedom of
inquiry. They appealed to conscience and reason as
they searched the Scriptures. Some of these scholar
preachers, such as Bernadino Ochino [we can add
Laelius and Faustus Socinus, Camilio Renato, and
Sebastian Castellio], reached a Unitarian Universalist
position not unlike that of American Universalists
George de Benneville and Hosea Ballou in the eighteenth and early nineteenth centuries.

However, this freedom was soon brought to an end by
the Inquisition. A number of these scholar preachers fled Italy
for Switzerland and Poland (The Commonwealth of Poland
and Lithuania), where they were influential in the liberal
anti-Trinitarian movement. Through their influence in Poland, for the first time in Europe, genuine toleration for all
faiths was instituted in 1557 at the Diet of Nobiliaries at
Warsaw and reaffirmed in 1573 with the protection of dissidents. Faustus Socinus, one such refugee from Italy, became a
leader of the Polish Brethren, a universalistic unitarian group,
later known as Socinians. Ferenz Dávid (known in the West

as Francis Dávid), who moved from Catholicism through Lutheranism and Calvinism to a universalistic unitarianism, became the great leader of the liberal Transylvanian movement. He was martyred in 1579 for his belief that only God, not Jesus, should be worshipped. The churches he influenced remain strong to this day as Unitarian churches in name.

Unitarianism and Universalism Come to America

In England, the beginnings of Unitarianism are associated with John Biddle, who was often persecuted and imprisoned for his Unitarian beliefs. He died in prison in 1662. Joseph Priestley, the discoverer of oxygen, was a major figure in eighteenth-century English Unitarianism. Both a Unitarian minister and a scientist, he voiced radical theological and political views and sympathized with the aims of the American and the French revolutions. In 1791, his meeting house and laboratory were destroyed by a mob outraged by his views. In 1794 Priestley immigrated to America and gave a series of lectures in the Universalist Church in Philadelphia when that city was still the capital of the United States. A number of leaders in the new nation attended these lectures, including Priestley's friend Thomas Jefferson. The lectures led to the founding of the First Unitarian Church of Philadelphia, the first permanently established church in the United States to take the Unitarian name.

Priestley had immigrated to Pennsylvania in 1794. Fifty-three years earlier, in 1741, George de Benneville, an important figure in early American Universalism, had come to the same state. De Benneville was an evangelistic lay preacher and a physician. In his boyhood, he had become convinced of the truth of Universalism. As a result of this conviction, he was ostracized by the French Protestant Church in England when he was fourteen.

Prior to coming to America, de Benneville preached the doctrine of universal salvation in Germany, England, Holland, and France. He was imprisoned in France and was saved from the guillotine by the intervention of King Louis XV. When he came to America, he was warmly welcomed by Pennsylvania pietist groups such as the Dunkers, the Universal Baptists, and the Quakers.

In the opinion of Unitarian Universalist minister and historian Clinton Lee Scott, George de Benneville is entitled to be called the founder of American Universalism. In *The Universalist Church of America: A Short History*, Scott reminds us,

> When Universalists today emphasize individual freedom of belief, the unrestricted use of reason, religion as a way of living, human beings and their welfare as central in organized life, truth as the only authority, the nurture of the inner spirit, and the Bible as one of the many forms of revelation, they are stressing principles which were central to the faith of the Spiritual Reformers. To leave this heritage out of consideration is to render difficult the understanding of the Universalism of the present day.

Of course these words apply to Unitarian Universalism as a whole. The past and the present have an organic, dynamic, living relationship to each other.

In 1759, *Union,* an important statement on Universalism by James Relly, was published in England. It became a target for ministers looking for heretics. A young man named John Murray heard Methodist ministers attacking Relly and resolved to approach him in person and bring the light to this heretic. But when he got to Relly, the tables were turned. James Relly proved to be a man of good conscience and strong persuasive powers. He convinced Murray of the soundness of the Universalist position. Murray became a Universalist.

Time spent in debtors' prison and the death of his wife and baby motivated Murray to come to America. It was not his intention to preach Universalism in his new country, but circumstances, as well as the depth of his beliefs, decreed otherwise. In 1770, he landed at Good Luck Point on Barnegat Bay, New Jersey, and was offered hospitality by Thomas Potter, a Universalist. At Potter's urging, Murray began to preach again. In 1779 he organized one of the first Universalist churches in America at Gloucester, Massachusetts. There, a group led by the merchant Winthrop Sargent, father of Judith Sargent Murray, had been studying Relly's *Union*. They invited John Murray to be their minister. Together, in 1786, they won a key legal battle for religious freedom in Massachusetts—the right to support the church and minister of their own choosing rather than pay taxes to support the congregationalist churches of the Standing Order.

Universalism had been developing in America even before Murray's arrival. There were de Benneville's efforts in Pennsylvania, along with Pennsylvania's radical spiritualists. Also, in the hill country of western Massachusetts and southern New Hampshire and Vermont, several congregations had broken away from the Baptists over the issue of universal salvation. The earliest leaders were Isaac Davis, August Streeter, and Caleb Rich, the latter organizing the first society of Universalists in 1773 in Warwick, Massachusetts. John Murray had limitless energy and the courage to spread the hopeful message of universal salvation in the face of the widely accepted, orthodox doctrine of eternal damnation for sinners. Thus Murray emerged as the main catalyst of a larger movement. He brought several of the first churches and leaders together in 1785 at Oxford, Massachusetts, including the Reverend Elhanan Winchester of Philadelphia. Their purpose was to organize this new denomination in order to bolster their legal struggle for religious freedom. They met yearly after that, and in 1790 leaders from several states gathered in Philadelphia to adopt a "Rule of Faith" and take a stand to "put an end to all wars" and slavery.

Although some of the oldest roots of our American Universalist and Unitarian movements can be traced to Pennsylvania in the second half of the eighteenth century, major events leading to the organization of American Unitarianism and Universalism took place in New England. Early in the eighteenth century, there were ministers in the Congregational churches who sowed the seeds of a more rational and liberal interpretation of the Christian faith. These men were characterized by great breadth of mind and spirit. Among them were Ebenezer Gay, who took a liberal stand on the doctrine of the Trinity as early as 1740, and Charles Chauncy and Jonathan Mayhew of Boston.

Chauncy, minister of the First Church in Boston, became a leader of the liberal wing of New England Congregationalists and wrote a book near the end of his life in 1787 defending universal salvation. Along with his younger colleague Jonathan Mayhew, minister of the West Church in Boston, Chauncy was an early supporter of liberty for the American colonies. Mayhew became the most eloquent early spokesperson and thinker for political and religious liberty in the colonies during the developing revolution. But as the years wore on, the conservatives proved increasingly intolerant of the growing number of Unitarian ministers, most of whom were graduates of the liberal Harvard Divinity School.

Organizing the Movements

William Ellery Channing, minister of the Federal Street Church in Boston and one of the greatest figures in American Unitar-

ian history, emerged as the leader of the liberal Congregationalists. "Unitarian Christianity," a sermon that he deliv-
ered in 1819 in Baltimore, Maryland, became the rallying
point for a new liberal religious movement and led to the
organization of the American Unitarian Association. The controversy affected many of the oldest churches in New England; out of the twenty-five oldest, twenty soon took the
Unitarian position. In all, approximately 125 churches became Unitarian and either withdrew or were forced from the
Congregational denomination. These churches were led by
men and women very much at home in the scientific and
literary currents of the day. Their ministers were for the most
part Harvard-educated.

With the Universalists, it was not a question of large
numbers of strong, established churches banding together to
form a new denomination. Ministers like Caleb Rich, John
Murray, Elhanan Winchester, and Hosea Ballou drew into
new congregations men and women who, like the Unitarians
within Congregationalism, sought a more liberal interpretation of Christianity. They came from different denominations. A very large number came from the Baptists and
some from the Methodists. They were for the most part self-
educated, less affluent, and more representative of the people
at large than the Unitarians of the period. In 1834, the Universalists made the Universalist General Convention their
national governing body, and in 1942 they adopted the name
The Universalist Church in America. The American Unitarian Association was organized in 1825.

While the Unitarians stressed free will and the potential
goodness of persons, the Universalists put more emphasis on
God as love. This led to the humorous but pertinent remark of
the nineteenth-century figure Thomas Starr King, son of a
Universalist minister, who, during his brief but brilliant ministry, had served both Universalist and Unitarian churches:

"The one [Universalist] thinks God is too good to damn them forever, and the other [Unitarian] thinks they are too good to be damned forever."

It is important to remember that our movement was born during a revolutionary period, and that the humanistic values of the period saturated the lives of our late eighteenth- and early nineteenth-century forebears. The links we had with the American Revolution are many. Suffice it to say that most of the signers of the Declaration of Independence were what we would today call "religious liberals."

One of our most precious inheritances is our congregational polity, which came to us from the Congregational churches and other churches of the free spirit. From the beginning it was accepted that ultimate decision-making power rests in the hands of the individual, autonomous churches. Local congregations select and ordain their ministers, determine their forms of worship or celebration, set their own requirements—or lack of requirements—for membership, and are responsible for all aspects of church government.

We have already seen that our beliefs change over the generations and that the beliefs of individuals differ within the same generation and the same congregation. One way to catch a glimpse of the ways in which our beliefs have changed and of the spirit and attitudes that unite us is to go directly to the words of those who set us on our way. Fortunately, what might be called the founding declarations have been brought together in two highly readable, well-edited books. *Universalism in America: A Documentary History of a Liberal Faith*, edited by Ernest Cassara, opens with a historical sketch and then presents selections from Universalist writings. Beginning with the writings of George de Benneville, it concludes with those of a contemporary Unitarian Universalist minister and poet, Kenneth L. Patton. A similar work, *The Epic of Unitarianism:*

Original Writings from the History of Liberal Religion, edited by David B. Parke, begins with selections from the writings of Michael Servetus and concludes with selections from the contemporary Unitarian Universalist scholar, theologian, and social reformer, James Luther Adams.

Opening Up Our Faith

Olympia Brown, suffragist pioneer in municipal reform, was ordained by the Northern (New York) Universalist Association in 1863. She is thus often spoken of as the first denominationally ordained woman minister in the United States. Another prominent Universalist woman was Judith Sargent Murray, an early American feminist writer. Of the Unitarians, Margaret Fuller, author of *Women in the Nineteenth Century,* is perhaps the best known. In his bicentennial historical essay on American Universalism, George Hunston Williams, Professor of Church History at Harvard University, writes, "Perhaps the most conspicuous feature of the Centennial Convention (the Universalist Centennial Convention held in Gloucester, Massachusetts, in 1870) was the prominence of women in the Universalist cause." To be a member of this company is to know that Unitarian Universalism is always reaching out and striving for greater understanding and inclusiveness.

Unitarians in Canada, by Phillip Hewett, minister emeritus of the Unitarian Church of Vancouver, British Columbia, was published in 1978. With scholarship, wit, and insight, Hewett describes the role Unitarians have played in Canadian life for more than 150 years. He brings to life our recent as well as more distant history within and outside Canada. His is one of a number of books that remind us of the depth and strength of our roots. The Unitarian Church in Montreal (Church of the Messiah) was organized in 1842, but the presence of Unitarians in the city had been known to the public as early as 1821. The Universalist Unitarian Church of Halifax was organized as a Universalist Church in 1843. The 1827 census listed fifty-five Universalists living in Nova Scotia. The First Unitarian Congregation of Toronto was organized in 1845. The Canadian Unitarian Council (Counseil Unitaire Canadien) was organized in 1961.

The Nineteenth Century and Beyond

In the 1830s, Unitarianism gave birth to the American cultural and religious movement known as Transcendentalism. This "New England Renaissance" gave a great impetus to American arts and philosophy. It influenced such writers as Emerson, Thoreau, Fuller, Hawthorne, Melville, Dickinson, and Whitman, to name the best known. Ralph Waldo Emerson, who was a Unitarian minister before branching out in his writing and lecturing, was one of its prime movers. He referred to Transcendentalism as "Idealism." Today we look back upon it as the beginning of a naturalism that sees the religious as centered in the everyday life experience.

Transcendentalists stressed the unity and miracle of daily life that transcends the dualisms of spirit and body, heaven and earth—as embodied in Emerson's writings and Walt Whitman's poetry. This naturalistic mysticism helps deepen the social activism at the center of our religious movement. In the years preceding the Civil War, much of the energy of Unitarians and Universalists in the United States was taken up with large issues such as the abolition of slavery, the emancipation of women, and the preservation of the Union.

After the war, it gradually became clear to Unitarians and Universalists that their survival and vibrancy depended on their capacity to bring their members together and find a stronger, renewed sense of conviction within our church as a whole. In a fascinating bicentennial essay published by the Universalist Historical Society in 1971, George Hunston Williams observes that in that 1870 General Convention, "Universalism completed the overhaul of its ecclesiastical structure, as did many other denominations after the Civil War, adopting a comprehensive new constitution for a uniform organization of the Universalist Church."

It has been a chronic problem for both Unitarians and Universalists to reconcile their love of individual freedom and autonomy with the necessity of church structures. There has been a strong bias against any kind of organization (particularly denominational), structure, or consensus on belief. In 1884, at a meeting of the National Conference of Unitarians, an event of great importance took place. The Unitarians transformed the American Unitarian Association from an association of individuals who paid annual dues of one dollar for voting privileges into an association of autonomous churches. This was done through the leadership of Henry W. Bellows, minister of the First Unitarian Church of New York City (now All Souls). Bellows was an organizing genius. During the Civil War, he had organized the United States Sanitary Commission to serve the war-wounded. Thomas Starr King, a close friend of Bellows, raised large amounts of money from wealthy Californians for the support of the Union and war relief. He also helped begin a movement toward closer relations between the Unitarians and the Universalists.

Our history teaches us that institutions, ideas, and beliefs are measured by the lives they help us lead. The Unitarians and the Universalists have had an excellent record in applying religious principles to the welfare of the world. Some of our activists include Susan B. Anthony, pioneer in the struggle for women's rights and anti-slavery leader; Adin Ballou, radical pacifist, severe critic of the injustices of capitalism, founder of Hopedale; Clara Barton, organizer of the American Red

Cross; Henry Bergh, one of the founders of the American Society for the Prevention of Cruelty to Children; Dorothea Dix, crusader for the reform of prisons and institutions for the mentally ill; Samuel Gridley Howe, pioneer in work with the blind; Horace Greeley, crusading newspaper editor, champion of labor unions and cooperatives; Thomas Starr King, minister of the First Unitarian Church of San Francisco, who helped save California for the Union through his powerful oratory and who, along with Father Junipero Serra, represents California in the Hall of Fame in Washington, DC; Abner Kneeland, advocate of land reform, public education, birth control, and communal living; Judith Sargent Murray and Margaret Fuller, intellectuals, essayists, and early feminists; Theodore Parker, abolitionist; and Joseph Tuckerman, pioneer social worker.

There was probably no movement in nineteenth-century America that had more of a humanitarian impact on society than the Unitarians and the Universalists. This activism has continued into the twentieth century. John Haynes Holmes, minister of the Community Church of New York City, an outspoken pacificist during World War I, was a co-founder of both the American Civil Liberties Union and the National Association for the Advancement of Colored People. He and Clarence Skinner, dean of the Universalist Theological School at Tufts University, helped start the so-called Community Church movement, which stresses social activism and ecumenicity. Jane Addams, celebrated social worker; John Dewey, signer of the Humanist Manifesto; Adlai Stevenson, politician; Whitney Young, Urban League leader; Sophia Lyon Fahs, pioneer in religious education; Stephen Fritchman, courageous minister of the First Unitarian Church of Los Angeles; and Dana Greeley, first president of the Unitarian Universalist Association and champion of civil rights, number among our most renowned figures. This is not to say that this road has been easy, or that there has been unanimity (unanimity has never been our strong point). But these reformers have represented the cutting edge. They have demonstrated that our religion is a powerful motivating force for both personal growth and social change.

It has not been our custom to reflect often on our history. We tend to be in a hurry to get things done and look forward rather than backward. But stopping to look at our past is reassuring, renewing, and energizing. It can also give us a sense of who we are, open up our minds to new ideas, and encourage us to deepen our religious life. Our story is adventurous and full of hope. Since Unitarian Universalists have attempted to keep alive the core teachings and beliefs of what has been called "the perennial religion," or universal teachings, our leaders have often been faced with persecution and charges of heresy, in the tradition of the prophets and seers of all ages. Discovering the depth and strength of these roots of ours is a nourishing experience that gives us the inspiration and stamina we need to meet today's great challenges.

Harry Scholefield and Paul Sawyer

Important Dates in Unitarian Universalist History

Early Christian History

225   Origen, one of the church Fathers, writes *On First Principles*, advocating belief in universal salvation.

325   Nicene Creed adopted at Council of Nicaea establishes dogma of the Trinity.

544   Belief in universal salvation condemned as heresy by a church council.

The Reformation

1511   Birth of Michael Servetus (the most famous of the sixteenth-century anti-Trinitarians).

1527   Martin Cellarius publishes *On the Works of God* (the earliest anti-Trinitarian book).

1531 Michael Servetus publishes *On the Errors of the Trinity*.

1553 Michael Servetus is burned at the stake in Geneva, Switzerland.

Polish Socinianism

1539 Birth of Faustus Socinus (leader of the Polish Socinian, or Polish Brethren, movement).

1546 Anti-Trinitarianism appears in Poland.

1557 Warsaw Diet of Nobiliaries legislates religious toleration.

1573 Reaffirmation of protections of dissidents by Diet and king.

1579 Faustus Socinus arrives in Poland.

1585 Founding of the Rakow press (the first official Unitarian press).

1591 The Socinian Church in Krakow is destroyed by a mob.

1658 The Polish Diet banishes Socinians.

Transylvanian (Hungarian) Unitarianism

1510 Birth of Francis Dávid (leader of Transylvanian Unitarians).

1566   Francis Dávid preaches against the doctrine of the Trinity.

1568   King John Sigismund (the Unitarian King) proclaims the earliest edict of complete religious toleration.

1579   Francis Dávid, condemned as a heretic, dies in prison.

1600   First official use of Unitarian name.

1821   English and Transylvanian Unitarians discover one another.

English Unitarianism and Universalism

1550   The Church of the Strangers is established in London.

1615   Birth of John Biddle (the founder of English Unitarianism).

1654   John Biddle is banished to the Scilly Isles.

1703   Thomas Emlyn is imprisoned at Dublin for anti-Trinitarian beliefs.

        Birth of George de Benneville (one of the leaders of American Universalism) in London.

1723   Birth of Theophilus Lindsey (one of the founders of the English Unitarian movement).

1733   Birth of Joseph Priestley (one of the greatest scientists of his age, the discoverer of oxygen, and a founder of both the English and American Unitarian movements).

1741   John Murray (the founder of American Universalism) born in Alton, England.

George de Benneville immigrates to Pennsylvania.

1750   James Relly, an associate of the evangelist George Whitefield, withdraws from this connection and establishes himself as an independent preacher of Universalism.

1759   *Union* (a theological treatise on universal salvation) by James Relly published in London.

1774   Essex Street Chapel opened in London (marking the beginning of permanently organized Unitarianism in England).

1791   Riots against Joseph Priestley and other Unitarians in Birmingham.

1794   Joseph Priestley immigrates to America.

1825   The British and Foreign Unitarian Association founded.

Canadian Unitarianism and Universalism

1832   First recorded meeting of Unitarians in Montreal.

1842   First permanent Unitarian church established in Montreal.

1843   A Universalist church established in Halifax.

1845   First Unitarian Church of Toronto established.

1891   An Icelandic-speaking Unitarian Church organized in Winnipeg. (Between 1891 and 1931, other Icelandic-speaking Unitarian Churches organized.)

1961   Canadian Unitarian Council organized.

1962   Canadian Unitarian Council/Conseil Unitaire Canadien relates itself officially to the UUA.

American Unitarianism and Universalism

1637   Samuel Gorton (a pioneer of Christian Universalism) driven out of Massachusetts for his political and religious radicalism.

1684   Joseph Gatchell has his tongue pierced with a red-hot iron for his statement, "All men should be saved."

1740   High point of the Great Awakening (whose emotional excesses stimulated a desire for a more rational religion).

1743   Christopher Sower (a Universalist Quaker), with the assistance of George de Benneville, prints the first Bible in America translated into German. Passages supporting the universal character of religion were printed in heavier type.

1770   John Murray arrives at Good Luck Point on Barnegat Bay, New Jersey.

On September 30, Murray preaches his first sermon in America in the meetinghouse of Thomas Potter.

1771   Birth of Universalist Hosea Ballou in Richmond, New Hampshire.

1774   John Murray preaches in Gloucester, Massachusetts.

1778   Caleb Rich organizes the General Society (Universalist) to ordain ministers and issue preaching licenses.

1779   Gloucester Universalists organize the first Universalist church in America and call John Murray as minister.

1785   Liturgy of King's Chapel Boston is revised, omitting references to the Trinity.

The first Universalist Convention (with delegates from churches) held in Oxford, Massachusetts.

1786   Gloucester Universalists successfully contest the right of the state to raise taxes for the established church.

A Universalist church (called the Universal Baptist Church) organized in Philadelphia.

1787   Congregation of King's Chapel, disregarding Episcopal procedures, ordains lay reader James Freeman as its minister, thereby becoming the first independent church of Unitarian beliefs.

1788   Murray wins the right of Universalists and dissenting ministers to be recognized as ordained ministers with authority to perform marriages.

1789   The Philadelphia Convention of Universalists adopts a declaration of faith and a set of principles of social reform.

1793   Second Universalist Convention in Oxford, Massachusetts, marks founding of precursor of Universalist Church in America.

1796   Joseph Priestley advocates Universalism and Unitarianism in Philadelphia. Founding of the First Unitarian Church of Philadelphia with encouragement of Priestley.

1802   The oldest Pilgrim church in America (founded at Plymouth in 1620) becomes Unitarian.

1803   Winchester Profession of Faith adopted by Universalists at Winchester, New Hampshire.

1805   Hosea Ballou writes *A Treatise on Atonement* (the first book published in America openly rejecting the doctrine of the Trinity).

Election of Henry Ware to Hollis Professor of Divinity at Harvard College begins Unitarian controversy.

1811   Harvard Divinity School established.

Maria Cook becomes first woman to preach a sermon in a Universalist pulpit.

1819   William Ellery Channing delivers his Baltimore sermon (a landmark statement of Unitarian principles).

The Christian Leader (Universalist) begins publication (originally named *The Universalist Magazine*).

1821   *The Christian Register* (Unitarian) begins publication.

1825   The American Unitarian Association (AUA) is organized.

1833   Formation of The General Convention of Universalists in the United States (with advisory powers only).

1836   Publication of first major Transcendentalist works.

1838   Ralph Waldo Emerson delivers "The Divinity School Address" (a major event in religious liberalism).

1840   Brook Farm founded by the Ripleys.

1841   Theodore Parker delivers his South Boston sermon "The Transient and Permanent in Christianity" (in defense of natural religion).

Adin Ballou founds Hopedale Community.

1844   Meadville Theological School established in Meadville, Pennsylvania.

1846   Adin Ballou's book, *Christian Non-Resistance*, advocating non-violence, influences Leo Tolstoy.

1847   The Universalist General Reform Association is organized.

1852   Tufts College founded by Universalists at Medford, Massachusetts.

1854   Publication of the first book under American Unitarian Association imprint—*Grains of God, or Select Thoughts on Sacred Themes* by the Reverend Cyrus A. Bartol, Jr.

1856   St. Lawrence University and Theological School founded by Universalists at Canton, New York.

1862   The Universalist Publishing House established.

1863   Ordination of Olympia Brown, arguably the first woman to be ordained by any denomination.

1865   The National Conference of Unitarian Churches organized.

1866   Organization of the Universalist General Convention (renamed in 1942 the Universalist Church of America).

1867   The Free Religious Association is organized.

1869   Women's Centenary Association formed (in 1939 became the Association of Universalist Women).

1880   The General Alliance of Unitarian and Other Liberal Christian Women (originally called Women's Auxiliary Conference) is organized.

1884   The American Unitarian Association becomes an association representative of and directly responsible to its member churches.

1889   Young People's Christian Union formed (later called Universalist Youth Fellowship).

Joseph Jordan ordained as first African-American Universalist minister.

1890   Universalists establish churches in Japan.

1896   Unitarian Young People's Religious Union organized.

1899   "Essential Principles of Universalism" adopted in Boston, Massachusetts.

First Merger Commission founded.

1900   The International Congress of Free Christians and Other Religious Liberals (today the International Association for Religious Freedom), the oldest international interfaith body, formed.

1902   Beacon Press launched (broadening the American Unitarian Association's publishing program) with publication of *Some Ethical Phases of the Labor Question*, by Carroll Wright.

1904   Starr King School for the Ministry founded in Berkeley, California, as Pacific Unitarian School of the Ministry.

1908   The Unitarian Fellowship for Social Justice organized.

1913   The General Sunday School Association organized at Utica, New York.

1917   The first denomination-wide Unitarian Youth Sunday held.

        Universalist General Convention adopts "Declaration of Social Principles" written by Clarence Skinner.

1920   The Unitarian Laymen's League organized.

1921   Universalist women acquire Clara Barton homestead (developed into camp for diabetic girls).

1931   Second Merger Commission.

1933   Free Church of America formed.

1934   Commission on Appraisal appointed by American Unitarian Association.

1935   Washington Statement of Faith adopted by Universalists.

1936   AUA Commission on Appraisal publishes *Unitarians Face a New Age*.

1937   The Unitarian Sunday School Society merged with the Religious Education Department of the American Unitarian Association.

        Frederick May Eliot elected president of the AUA; Sophia Lyon Fahs appointed children's editor.

1938   The Beacon Press pioneers a series of publications in religious education.

1939   Unitarian Service Committee organized.

1941   Young People's Christian Union reorganized into Universalist Youth Fellowship.

1942   The Young People's Religious Union reorganized into American Unitarian Youth.

        The Universalist General Convention renamed the Universalist Church of America.

1943   The Unitarian Service Committee makes plans for medical missions to war-devastated countries.

1944   The Church of the Larger Fellowship organized to serve Unitarians living in areas without Unitarian churches.

1945   The Universalist Service Committee formed.

1948   Continental program to establish Unitarian fellowships begun.

1949   Charles Street Meeting House in Boston, Massachusetts, initiated by American Universalists.

1950   American and English Unitarians jointly celebrate the 125th anniversary of their respective denominational organizations.

1953   Liberal Religious Youth, Inc., is formed by the merger of American Unitarian Youth and Universalist Youth Fellowship.

The Council of Liberal Churches (Universalist-Unitarian), Inc., is organized for the federation of the departments of publications, education, and public relations.

The Christian Leader renamed *The Universalist Leader.*

1956   Unitarians and Universalists create Joint Commission on Merger to examine feasibility of merging the two denominations.

1958   *The Christian Register* renamed *The Unitarian Register.*

1961   The American Unitarian Association and the Universalist Church of America officially consolidate and organize the Unitarian Universalist Association.

The Unitarian Register and *The Universalist Leader* are merged as the Unitarian Universalist *Register-Leader.*

1962   The Unitarian Laymen's League and the National Association of Universalist Men join to form the Laymen's League (Unitarian Universalist).

1963   The Alliance of Unitarian Women and the Association of Universalist Women join to form the Unitarian Universalist Women's Federation.

The Unitarian Service Committee and the Department of World Service of the Unitarian Universalist Association unite to form the Unitarian Universalist Service Committee, Inc.

First General Assembly resolution in support of abortion rights.

1964   First resolution against the Vietnam War passed by a General Assembly.

1965   James Reeb, Unitarian Universalist minister, murdered in Selma, Alabama, in civil rights protest organized by Martin Luther King, Jr. As a result, protest intensifies across the nation. UUA Board adjourns in the middle of its meeting and moves meeting site to Selma.

1966   Martin Luther King, Jr., delivers Ware Lecture at General Assembly.

1967   Black Unitarian Universalist Caucus organized.

1970   *Unitarian Universalist World* succeeds *Register-Leader*.

1971   *About Your Sexuality* curriculum for junior high youth published.

1972   Beacon Press publishes *Pentagon Papers,* and the federal government investigates UUA bank records.

1973   Federal judge dismisses UUA Pentagon Papers Case without prejudice after U.S. Attorney's statement that the investigation would not be resumed.

1979   Death of UUA President Paul Carnes; election of President O. Eugene Pickett.

1983   Young Religious Unitarian Universalists (YRUU) succeeds Liberal Religious Youth (LRY).

1985   Election of President William F. Schulz.

$20,000,000 endowment given to the UUA by the North Shore Unitarian Universalist Society of Plandome, New York.

1987   Tabloid *Unitarian Universalist World* becomes the *World*, publishing in magazine format.

$9,000,000 grant for theological education given to UUA by the North Shore Unitarian Universalist Society of Plandome, New York.

1989   UUA delegation seeking guarantees of religious freedom enters Romania two weeks after the revolution.

Partner church program established between UUA and Transylvanian congregations.

1991   More than 400 ministers sign *New York Times* ad opposing Persian Gulf War.

1992   First meeting of the World Summit of Unitarian Leaders in Budapest, Hungary.

Beacon Press publishes bestselling book *The Measure of Our Success* by Marian Wright Edelman. Beacon author Mary Oliver wins National Book Award for poetry.

1993   Denise Taft Davidoff elected UUA moderator; John A. Buehrens elected president.

International Council of Unitarians and Universalists organized.

1994   *Journey Toward Wholeness* report commits the UUA to a long-term struggle against racism and other forms of oppression and to a more inclusive and multicultural future.

1996   General Assembly calls for civil marriage for same-sex couples.

1997   Davidoff and Buehrens re-elected.

Four-year "Fulfilling the Promise" process of covenantal renewal begun.

1999   UUA introduces *Our Whole Lives* sexuality education curriculum.

2000   William G. Sinkford is elected UUA president, the first African American to head a traditionally white denomination.

2003   Boston General Assembly is the largest in history, with more than 7,700 in attendance. Julian Bond delivers the Ware Lecture.

2003-   Significant UU public witness supporting marriage
2004   equality for same-sex couples.

About the
Unitarian Universalist Association

The Unitarian Universalist Association is simply the coming together of over 1,000 free liberal religious congregations for a common purpose: to support the vitality and growth of congregations, to start new congregations, and to promote the principles that we share in the wider world. The Association was formed in 1961 when the congregations of the American Unitarian Association and the Universalist Church of America decided to join together as one religious community. Today the Association serves more than 200,000 adults and children in the United States, as well as congregations in several countries around the world.

The Association's policy-setting body is its General Assembly, which meets annually and is made up of delegates from the churches and fellowships. The General Assembly makes overall policy for carrying out the Association's purposes, reviews the program, and elects for stated terms a president, a moderator, a financial advisor, and four other members of the Board of Trustees. Twenty members of the Board are elected from districts. The Board conducts the affairs of the Association and carries out its policies and directives as provided by law.

The congregations that make up the Association are self-governing and made up of individuals and families who choose to become members. Congregational members join in a covenant in which they promise one another how they will walk together as they live out their mission and ministry in the world. Congregational membership is open to all, regardless of color, race, sex, ability, sexual orientation, age, or national origin. Specific religious beliefs are not required. Openness and attention to the individual's personal spiritual journey are central.

Nationally, the Association is organized into twenty-one geographic districts. Each district serves the congregations in its area with a variety of programs and promotes increased participation in the life of the denomination. Professional staff from the UUA and the districts offer counsel and assistance in many matters to districts, area councils or "clusters," and individual congregations.

Among the many functions and services of the Association are the following: aiding Unitarian Universalist congregations, organizing new groups, encouraging area leadership, providing building loans, producing pamphlets and devotional materials, keeping more than 100,000 Unitarian Universalist families informed with issues of the *UU World* magazine, creating a sense of national unity and purpose, maintaining interfaith relationships, providing financial advice, managing an investment trust, creating religious education curricula, exchanging information on social action, supporting a Unitarian Universalist voice in Washington, accrediting men and women for the ministry, assisting congregations to find new ministers, and raising funds to accomplish and sustain the many programs of the Association. Beacon Press is a non-profit publisher dedicated to the responsible exploration of the human condition; over half a million Beacon Press books are sold each year. Skinner House Books, an imprint of the UUA, publishes books especially for Unitarian Universalists; Skinner House has more than one hundred titles in print, including this *Pocket Guide.*

Many (but by no means all) Unitarian Universalist ministers receive their theological education at one of three schools: Meadville Lombard Theological School, affiliated with the University of Chicago; Starr King School for the Ministry in Berkeley, California; and Harvard (University) Divinity School in Cambridge, Massachusetts.

A number of organizations related to the Association address specific constituencies. These include the Unitarian Universalist Service Committee, the Unitarian Universalist Women's Federation, Young Religious Unitarian Universalists, Diverse and Revolutionary Unitarian Universalist Multicultural Ministries, the Unitarian Universalist United Nations Office, professional organizations (for ministers, religious educators, administrators, and musicians), and many more.

Unitarian and Unitarian Universalist congregations in Canada are served by the Canadian Unitarian Council. National groups of Unitarian and Unitarian Universalist congregations have joined together to form the International Council of Unitarians and Universalists. Many U.S. congregations are in relationship with congregations from other nations (especially the historic Unitarian congregations of Transylvania) through the Partner Church Program.

The Association is an active participant in the interfaith dialogue in the United States through the Interfaith Alliance and other organizations, as well as supporting international interfaith collaboration through the International Association for Religious Freedom (IARF) and Religions for Peace. Through our Holdeen India Program, the Association supports the empowerment of women and justice for the Dalit ("Untouchable") cast in India.

For further information on the Unitarian Universalist Association and related organizations, write to the UUA, 25 Beacon Street, Boston, Massachusetts 02108-2800. Call us at (617) 742-2100 or email us at info@uua.org. You can also reach us online at www.uua.org.

About the
Church of the Larger Fellowship

The Church of the Larger Fellowship (CLF) provides a ministry to isolated religious liberals who, for geographical or other reasons, are unable to attend a Unitarian Universalist congregation. CLF offers them a spiritual home within the Unitarian Universalist movement.

By mail, phone, email, and fax, CLF serves a worldwide network of more than 3,000 members, including over 400 families with children and young people. Members live in some fifty-nine countries, all fifty of the United States, and all the Canadian provinces. Women and men around the globe who cherish liberal religious convictions find a warm welcome, spiritual inspiration, personal pastoral support, religious education, and a variety of practical resources in this church without walls."

CLF sends *Quest*, its monthly publication containing articles and sermons from Unitarian Universalist perspectives as well as CLF and Unitarian Universalist news, to each member. (*Quest* is also available on audiotape.) In addition, members receive the *UU World*, the bi-monthly magazine published by the Unitarian Universalist Association.

The church has its own full-time minister who is available to members for personal support and counseling, religious and theological discussions, and practical help. The minister's 24-hour, toll-free "800" line enables members to contact the minister directly as needed.

CLF maintains a small loan library of denominational resource materials adapted for home use. Library holdings include books on Unitarian Universalist history and theology; Month of Sundays (sets of four complete worship services in large print); video- and audiotaped Unitarian Universalist sermons; adult self-study courses; and religious education curricula for children and youth. The church's director of religious education is available to consult with members about these resources and other religious education questions.

CLF also offers a program for small churches and fellowships that are experiencing a need for programming help and support, particularly with weekly worship and religious education programs for children. Called "Church-on-Loan," the program provides enrolled groups with professional guidance and access to a varied set of worship and religious tools from the CLF Loan Library resources. "Church OnLine" is a new component of Church-on-Loan, with worship and religious education resources available online for small groups around the world.

The need for a "church from a distance" emerged early in the history of the United States. In 1825 Thomas Jefferson wrote to Dr. Benjamin Waterhouse, "The population of my neighborhood is too slender and is too much divided into other sects to maintain any one preacher well. I must therefore be contented to be a Unitarian by myself." Later, in 1884, "The Post-Office Mission" was organized. CLF is the legal and logical successor carrying on this church-by-mail.

First organized in 1944 under the auspices of the American Unitarian Association, CLF was incorporated in 1970 as an autonomous organization. The church is managed by its own board of directors, which is elected by and responsible to CLF members. A "member canvass" is held each fall to meet the expense budget; members pledge according to their commitment and ability to contribute. Members are also asked to support the UUA's Annual Program Fund.

To assist in meeting expenses, an endowment fund honoring Frederick May Eliot, a leader in the Unitarian Universalist movement, and Clinton Lee Scott, a founding minister, creates a perpetual foundation. In addition, CLF has a "Society of Sponsors"—individuals, many of whom are members and/or ministers of existing churches and fellowships, who recognize the service that CLF provides to the movement and contribute toward its mission. Not only does CLF introduce liberal religion to hundreds of new people each year, but many new congregations emerge from a nucleus of CLF members.

For further information about the Church of the Larger Fellowship, write to CLF, 25 Beacon Street, Boston, Massachusetts 02108-2823. Call us at (617) 948-6166, email us at clf@uua.org, or visit us online at http://www.clfuu.org.

Resources

BOOKS

Some of these titles are out of print. Consult your public or church library regarding availability. Titles marked with an * may be available for purchase from the UUA Bookstore: 25 Beacon Street, Boston, Massachusetts 02108-2800; telephone (800) 215-9076, http://www.uua.org.

*Beach, George Kimmich. *Questions for the Religious Journey: Finding Your Own Path.* Boston: Skinner House, 2002.

*Beard, Margaret L., and Roger W. Comstock, eds. *All Are Chosen: Stories of Lay Ministry and Leadership.* Boston: Skinner House, 1998.

*Bowens-Wheatley, Marjorie, and Nancy Palmer Jones, eds. *Soul Work: Anti-racist Theologies in Dialogue.* Skinner House Books, 2002.

*Buehrens, John A., and Forrest Church. *A Chosen Faith: An Introduction to Unitarian Universalism.* 2nd ed. Boston: Beacon Press, 1998.

*Cassara, Ernest. *Universalism in America.* 2nd ed. Boston: Skinner House, 1997.

Chryssides, George D. *The Elements of Unitarianism.* Boston: Element, 1998.

*Collier, Kenneth W. *Our Seven Principles in Story and Verse: A Collection for Children and Adults.* Boston: Skinner House, 1997.

*Emerson, Dorothy May, ed. *Standing Before Us: Unitarian Universalist Women and Social Reform, 1776-1936.* Boston: Skinner House, 1999.

*Essex Conversations Coordinating Committee. *Essex Conversations: Visions for Lifespan Religious Education.* Boston: Skinner House, 2001.

*Frost, Edward A., ed. *With Purpose and Principle: Essays About the Seven Principles of Unitarian Universalism.* Boston: Skinner House, 1998.

*Grohsmeyer, Janeen K. *A Lamp in Every Corner: Our Unitarian Universalist Storybook.* Boston: Unitarian Universalist Association, 2004.

Hitchings, Catherine. *Universalist and Unitarian Women Ministers.* Boston: Unitarian Universalist Historical Society, 1985.

*Howe, Charles A. *The Larger Faith: A Short History of American Universalism.* Boston: Skinner House, 1993.

*Marshall, George N. *Challenge of a Liberal Faith*. 3rd ed. Boston: Skinner House, 1987.

*Mendelsohn, Jack. *Being Liberal in an Illiberal Age: Why I Am a Unitarian Universalist*. Boston: Skinner House, 1995.

Miller, Russell E. *The Larger Hope: History of the Universalist Church in America*. 2 Vols. Boston: Unitarian Universalist Historical Society, 1979-1985.

*Morrison-Reed, Mark D. *Black Pioneers in a White Denomination*. 3rd ed. Boston: Skinner House, 1994.

*Owen-Towle, Tom. *Freethinking Mystics With Hands: Exploring the Heart of Unitarian Universalism*. Boston: Skinner House, 1998.

*_____. *Growing a Beloved Community: Twelve Hallmarks of a Healthy Congregation*. Boston: Skinner House Books, 2004.

*Parke, David, ed. *The Epic of Unitarianism*. Boston: Skinner House, 1980.

Patton, Kenneth. *A Religion for One World*. Boston: Beacon Press, 1976.

*Robinson, David. *The Unitarians and the Universalists*. Westport, Connecticut: Greenwood Press, 1985.

*Ross, Warren R. *The Premise and the Promise: The Story of the Unitarian Universalist Association*. Boston: Skinner House Books, 2001.

Schulz, William F. *Finding Time and Other Delicacies.* Boston: Skinner House, 1992.

Scott, Clinton Lee. *The Universalist Church of America: A Short History.* Boston: Universalist Historical Society, 1957.

Wilbur, Earl Morse. *Our Unitarian Heritage.* Boston: Beacon Press, 1956.

*Wright, Conrad. ed. *A Stream of Light: A Sesquicentennial History of American Unitarianism.* Boston: Skinner House, 1975.

*_____. *The Unitarian Controversy: Essays on American Unitarian History.* Boston: Skinner House, 1994.

_____. ed. *American Unitarianism, 1805-1865.* Boston: Northeastern University Press, 1989.

PERIODICALS

For subscriptions to periodicals, write directly to these addresses.

Ferment
The young adult newsletter from the UUA office of Young Adult and Campus Ministry. 25 Beacon Street, Boston, Massachusetts 02108-2800. www.uua.org/ya-cm/resources/ferment.html

Synapse
The newspaper of the Young Religious Unitarian Universalists. www.uua.org/YRUU/synapse. YRUU, 25 Beacon Street, Boston, Massachusetts 02108-2800.

UU World
The official journal of the Unitarian Universalist Association.
25 Beacon Street, Boston, MA 02108-2800. www.uuworld.org

PAMPHLETS

Contact the UUA Bookstore to inquire about these and other pamphlets.

Introductions

Becoming a Member
Journeys: The Many Paths to Unitarian Universalism
Meet the Unitarian Universalists
Our Unitarian Universalist Faith: Frequently Asked Questions
We Are Unitarian Universalists
Welcome to Unitarian Universalism: A Community of Truth,
    Service, Holiness and Love
Worship in Unitarian Universalist Congregations

Children and Youth

Faith Without a Creed
Love Remembers: Helping Kids Heal After a Death
UU Religious Education and Your Child
Youth on Fire

Diversity

Can We Find a Home Here? Answering Questions of Interfaith
    Couples

Soulful Journeys: The Faith of African American Unitarian Universalists

Unitarian Universalism: A Religious Home for Bisexual, Gay, Lesbian, and Transgender People

Perspectives

Choices in Dying

Discovering Unitarian Universalism from Catholic and Jewish Perspectives

Engagement with the World: A Personal Perspective of Faith in Action

Is Our Church Gay? Answering Children's Questions About Homophobia and Sexual Orientation

Spirituality: Unitarian Universalist Experiences

History

The Flaming Chalice

Unitarian Universalist Origins: Our Historic Faith

"UU Views" Series

Unitarian Universalist Views of the Bible

Unitarian Universalist Views of Church

Unitarian Universalist Views of Faith in the Workplace

Unitarian Universalist Views of God

Unitarian Universalist Views of Jesus

Unitarian Universalist Views of Prayer

ADDITIONAL RESOURCES

Other materials are available from these sources.

Diverse and Revolutionary Unitarian Universalist
Multicultural Ministries (DRUUMM)
1320 18th Street, NW, Suite 300B
Washington, DC 20036

Interweave
c/o Jane Dwinell
167 Milk Street, #406
Boston, MA 02109

Latino/a Unitarian Universalist Networking Association
(LUUNA)
c/o Rev. José Ballester
46 Greentree Lane, #13
South Weymouth, MA 02190

Unitarian Universalist Service Committee, 130 Prospect
Street, Cambridge, Massachusetts 02139-1845.

Unitarian Universalist United Nations Office, 777 UN
Plaza, Suite C-C, New York, New York 10017.

Unitarian Universalist Women's Federation, 25 Beacon
Street, Boston, Massachusetts 02108-2800.

*A large and varied stock of books, pamphlets, and teacher resources
relating to Unitarian Universalism are listed in the UUA Bookstore
catalog. For a free copy, call or write the UUA Bookstore, 25 Beacon
Street, Boston, Massachusetts 02108-2800; (617) 742-2100, ext.
101 or 102; uua.org/bookstore.*